Propellerhead Record™

IGNITE!

The Visual Guide for New Users

Michael Prager

COURSE TECHNOLOGY
CENGAGE Learning™

Australia • Brazil • Japan • Korea • Mexico • Singapore • Spain • United Kingdom • United States

Propellerhead Record™ Ignite!
Michael Prager

**Publisher and General Manager,
Course Technology PTR:**
Stacy L. Hiquet

Associate Director of Marketing:
Sarah Panella

Manager of Editorial Services:
Heather Talbot

Marketing Manager: Mark Hughes

Executive Editor: Mark Garvey

Project Editor and Copy Editor:
Kim Benbow

Technical Reviewer: G.W. Childs

Interior Layout: Jill Flores

Cover Designer: Mike Tanamachi

**Indexer: BIM Indexing &
Proofreading Services**

Proofreader: Michael Beady

For product information and technology assistance, contact us at
Cengage Learning Customer & Sales Support, 1-800-354-9706.

For permission to use material from this text or product,
submit all requests online at **cengage.com/permissions.**
Further permissions questions can be e-mailed to
permissionrequest@cengage.com.

Record, Reason, ReWire, REX, and ReGroove are trademarks of Propellerhead Software AB, Stockholm, Sweden.

Microsoft, Windows, and Internet Explorer are either registered trademarks or trademarks of Microsoft Corporation in the United States and/or other countries.

All other trademarks are the property of their respective owners.

All images © Cengage Learning unless otherwise noted.

Library of Congress Control Number: 2009942401

ISBN-13: 978-1-4354-5560-3

ISBN-10: 1-4354-5560-6

Course Technology, a part of Cengage Learning
20 Channel Center Street
Boston, MA 02210
USA

Cengage Learning is a leading provider of customized learning solutions with office locations around the globe, including Singapore, the United Kingdom, Australia, Mexico, Brazil, and Japan. Locate your local office at: **international.cengage.com/region.**

Cengage Learning products are represented in Canada by Nelson Education, Ltd. For your lifelong learning solutions, visit **courseptr.com.**

Visit our corporate Web site at **cengage.com.**

Printed in the United States of America
1 2 3 4 5 6 7 12 11 10

I would like to dedicate this book to my mother and father.
Your love, courage, bravery, and strength are immeasurable.
Both of you are a true inspiration to those all around you,
and I am honored to be your son. I love you both very much.

Acknowledgments

I'd like to thank the following people and organizations for their help in making this book possible. First and foremost, Propellerhead Software: modern music would not be as cool without your groundbreaking programs. Thanks also to Line6 for their ingenious amp modeling. Thanks to G.W. Childs and Kim Benbow for their editing expertise. Thanks to Mark Garvey and all of the folks at Cengage Learning for their guidance and help throughout the creation of this book. Thanks to my family at Guitar Center Management. A special thanks, as always, goes to my wife Jeannie. I would also like to thank my friends and family for their love, support, and above all, their patience.

And as always, I thank you for picking up this book. I hope you have as much fun using Record as I do.

About the Author

Michael Prager has been involved with music technology for 15 years and has worked for such companies as Guitar Center Management, Cakewalk, Steinberg, Disney Interactive, Spectrasonics, Q Up Arts, Sony Classical, the Columbia College Hollywood, and *Keyboard* magazine. Michael has worked on various ArtistPro instructional DVDs and is the author of several books and CD-ROMs from Course Technology PTR, including *Reason 4 Power!*, *Sampling and Soft Synth Power!*, *Mac Home Recording Power!*, *Reason CSi Starter*, and *Reason CSi Master*.

Contents

} Introduction

Welcome to the exciting world of Record by Propellerhead Software. If you have been looking for a great piece of recording software that's easy to use and has a fantastically dynamic graphic interface, then Record is a great choice. This program has everything you need to start recording your music right away and includes all of the tricks of the trade required to make your music sound like it was recorded and mixed in an big expensive studio with very little effort. Additionally, Record has many bonus features that you simply won't find anywhere else.

Think of Record as the sequel to Propellerhead's already popular Reason software, which is one of the most widely used music creation applications in the music industry. Its robust features and slick interface, combined with an arsenal of software synths and drums machines, makes it a force to be reckoned with. However, the one thing that Reason didn't do was record audio tracks. So if you wanted to record your voice or guitar into your computer, you would need to turn to another program, such as Pro Tools, Cubase, Logic, or SONAR.

But it was only a matter of time before Propellerhead would throw its hat in the ring and give its masses a ground-breaking recording program that stayed true to the layout and functionality their users have come to expect. And man, oh man have they hit the nail on the head! Record delivers everything you need:

 ❊ Virtually limitless tracks of audio
 ❊ Effects and EQs
 ❊ Quick-and-easy editing
 ❊ Adaptable routing capabilities
 ❊ Advanced integration with Reason
 ❊ And so much more!

At the end of the day, Record is ready and waiting to help you channel your creativity.

So what's the purpose of *Propellerhead Record Ignite!* and what you can expect from this book? If you open these pages expecting to find in-depth discussions on algorithms, bit depths, sampling rates, and time code, you've probably come to the wrong place. This book is intended to be used as a beginner's guide to using Record. The point is to quickly get you up and running with Record in as little time as possible. Within these pages, you'll find exercises that will introduce you to new concepts and how to achieve your goals quickly. I'll cover all of the biggies, including installation, recording your first track, using effects, basic editing, using MIDI, and publishing your songs. In other words, you'll find instant success with little fuss.

Cengage Learning also publishes another line of books called the Power! series, and you can bet the upcoming *Propellerhead Record Power!* book will answer all of the tech geek questions and expand on the basic concepts covered in this book. As I have written a few Power! books myself, I can tell you that everything you want to know about Record, right down to the zeros and ones, can be found there.

Now that you have a handle on what's going to be covered, let's jump in and start recording!

Companion Website Downloads

You may download the companion website files from www.courseptr.com/downloads. Enter the book's ISBN in the Companion Search field.

1 } Installation, Authorization, and Preferences

Welcome to the beginning of what is sure to be an exciting and creative adventure in the world of Propellerhead Software's Record. This book is going to quickly become your go-to guide for using Record and digging into some of the groundbreaking features within. Throughout this book, you'll find quick yet effective exercises paired with explanations and concepts that should make learning this program a snap. Before you know it, you'll be rockin' through Record like a blistering fast guitar solo.

Before digging in, you need to install Record, authorize it, and set up the preferences. Doing this correctly will help you realize the true potential of Record with minimum technical issues. If you have already installed Record and authorized it, you can jump ahead to the "Setting Your Preferences" section to learn how to set those.

Installing Record

Installing Record is pretty simple and straightforward. You just need the free hard drive space and a bit of time, as the program installs from a DVD. Before you get started, just make sure that you have the following items:

※ The Record DVD

※ The Ignition Key—This is the USB hardware key that comes included in the box.

※ The Product Authorization Card

It probably would be a good idea to have an Internet connection handy as well, as you will need to register Record online at the Propellerhead website.

Although the installation of Record looks a little different between Mac OSX and Windows, they are both relatively easy and straight-forward. Just install Record as you would any other program.

One thing to note here is that Record 1.0 works on the latest Apple and Microsoft operating systems, which means if you want to use Record with a Mac running Snow Leopard or a PC running Windows 7, there's no problem with this.

Once you finish installing Record, it's a good idea to restart your computer.

Register Record Now!

Before authorizing Record, you should launch your Internet browser and register your copy of Record at the Propellerhead Software website (www.propellerhead.se). You'll need to have the Production Authorization Card handy. Doing this now will make the authorization process a little quicker, not to mention getting access to technical support and updates for Record should you need them.

Authorizing Record

There are many DAW software applications on the market, and each of them uses various forms of copy protection. Some use hard-ware keys (aka *dongles*), some of them use challenge/response codes, and some just require a serial number the first time you run the application. I am a pretty big advocate for copy protection, as it is necessary for software developers to protect their intellectual property. At the same time, a copy protection that's too restrictive can lead to complications, especially when you're trying to just power up, plug in, and make some music. That's the whole idea of using these programs, isn't it?

One of the things that I really like about Record is that it has one of the most flexible authorization schemes around. When you launch Record for the first time, you'll see three ways to authorize and use Record:

1 Run in Demo Mode—If you don't have either your Ignition Key or an Internet connection, no problem. You can run Record in Demo mode, which allows you to launch Record, record your tracks, and save your work. However, you cannot export your song to an audio file, and you can't open any already saved Record songs, with the exception of the demo song.

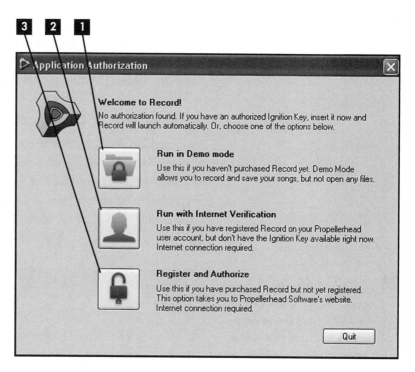

2 Run with Internet Verification—This is extremely useful if you don't have the Ignition Key handy. All you need is an Internet connection to authorize the program as you launch it.

3 Register and Authorize—This is the option for the USB key, or dongle. All you need to do is plug this in, and Record will launch.

At this point, let's use the Ignition Key. Insert it into an available USB slot and Record will automatically launch.

Setting Your Preferences

Once Record has been authorized and has launched, the Setup Wizard appears. This is used to help guide you through the steps of setting up your audio and MIDI hardware. While I find that this is a pretty useful function of Record, I feel that learning the Preferences window is generally a better idea, as you will most likely need to make adjustments to your preferences again down the road. That said, I'll use the Preferences window for this example.

Select Edit > Preferences if you are using Windows or Record > Preferences if you are using a Mac. This will launch the Preferences window, which will be set to the default General page under the Page drop-down list. Click on this list and select the Audio page.

Setting Up Your Audio Interface

The first thing you'll want to do in the Preferences window is set up your audio interface. If you're new to audio applications, an audio interface is the external USB or FireWire device used for connecting microphones, speakers, and so on. Some examples include Digidesign M-Box 2 and PreSonus FirePod.

1 First, select an audio interface of your choice by **clicking** on the **Audio Card Driver drop-down list**. As you can see, I have an audio interface option called ASIO Audio Kontrol 1. This is the audio interface I'll use throughout most of this book. When you're doing this, you might see other drivers to select, such as Core Audio, DX, WDM, or MME. As you are probably new to this, I would suggest using either the ASIO or Core Audio driver for the best performance.

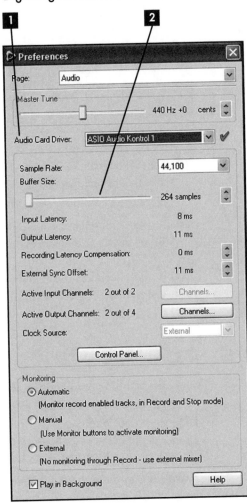

2 Next, you will want to **make adjustments** to your *latency*, which is simply a term that defines the delay between playing a note on your instrument and hearing it play back through your speakers. You'll want this to be on the lower side, anywhere between 256 to 512 samples should do it. This is possible either by using the slider located just under the Buffer Size option or if you're using an ASIO driver, you'll need to click on the Control Panel button to adjust the latency. Once you make the proper adjustments, the Input and Output latency (measured in milliseconds) will be displayed just below the slider.

Setting Up Your MIDI Keyboard

The last preference you're going to set up is your MIDI keyboard so that you can play the virtual instruments that come with Record. I'll assume that you are familiar with MIDI and how MIDI works. Select the Keyboards and Control Surfaces page and let's begin.

1 **Click** on the **Auto-Detect Surfaces button**. This will tell Record to scan your computer to see if you have any MIDI keyboards or control surfaces connected. Assuming that you have a keyboard connected, you should see it listed as an attached surface.

2 If you have multiple keyboards or control surfaces connected, make sure that you **select one** of them by clicking on it in the **Attached Surfaces dialog box** and then select Make Master Keyboard. This tells Record to listen only to the selected device when receiving MIDI messages.

3 **Close** the **Preferences window**.

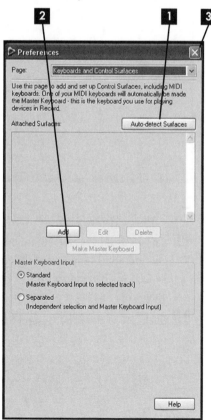

In some cases, Record will not be able to detect your keyboard. This could be due to its age or various other reasons. This isn't a problem though, as you can still set up your keyboard as a controller for Record by clicking on the Add button and following these steps:

1 Select a **manufacturer** from the drop-down list. If you're not sure of the manufacturer or it is not listed, then select Other.

2 Select a **model** from the drop-down list. If you selected a specific manufacturer, you will probably see it listed here. If you selected Other as the manufacturer, then you will need to specify what kind of keyboard controller it is.

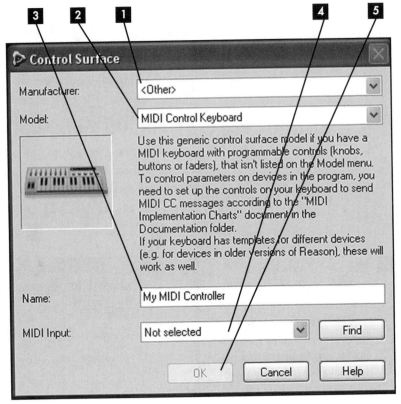

3 Give the keyboard controller a **name** in the Name field.

4 Select the **MIDI input** that the keyboard controller is connected to. If you are not sure, you can click on the Find button, at which point Record will ask you to press a key or move a knob on the keyboard controller. Record should then automatically locate the MIDI input.

5 Click OK to close the Control Surface window.

What if you don't have a MIDI keyboard, but you still want to play the cool sounds of Record? Not a problem; Record has your back. Select the On Screen Piano Keys option from the Window menu. Record will let you use your computer keyboard to trigger virtual instruments, so no MIDI keyboard is needed to start using Record. However, having a keyboard will only make your experience all the better.

Now that you've installed Record and set up your preferences, let's get to know the Record interface.

2 } Getting to Know Record

The first time you launch Record and have a look at the main screen of the program, it can look a little daunting to say the least. Even if you're a seasoned user of Reason, the Record interface is a bit more in depth. Oh sure, there are commonalities, as is the case with any DAW program, but Record still has a lot of power under the hood and includes a lot of features you simply won't find in many other applications. So, let's get started. The first thing you want to do is open up the Record Demo Song, which is a catchy tune written and recorded by the Baguettes. Navigate to the File menu and select Open Demo Song > The Baguettes—We Get It On. The song should load up in few seconds. If you want to start and stop the song, use the spacebar on your computer keyboard.

The first thing to notice is that the Record interface is divided into four different areas:

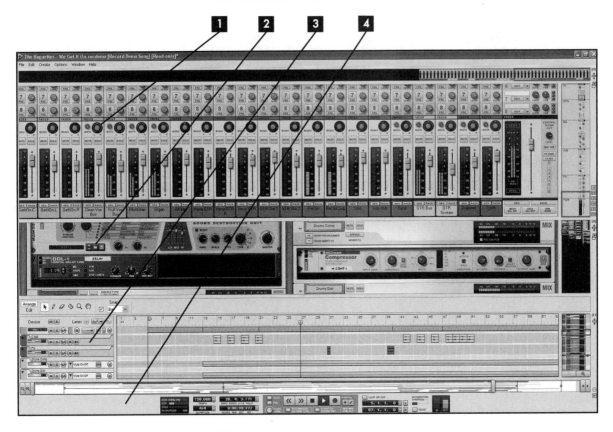

1. The Main Mixer—This is where you make your adjustments to volume, panning, and effects.

2. The Rack—This is where you create all of your instruments, effects, and mixer channels for your song.

3. The Sequencer—This is where you record your audio tracks, virtual instrument tracks, and automation. It is read in a linear fashion from left to right.

4. The Transport Panel—This is where you stop, start, rewind, and fast-forward your Record song. Additionally, you set your tempo, time signature, and loop point, among other things.

Each of these areas can be resized by simply clicking and dragging up and down on one the dividers between each area. Additionally, you can maximize an area by using either the Maximize button located in the upper-right corner of each area or by using the following key commands:

❈ F5—This will maximize and restore the Main Mixer.

❈ F6—This will maximize and restore the Rack.

❈ F7—This will maximize and restore the Sequencer.

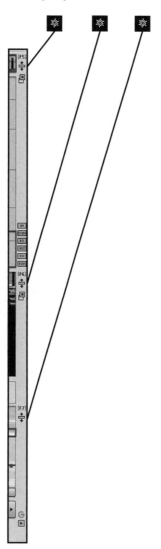

Please note that the Transport Panel will not resize, but it can be shown and hidden by using the Show/Hide Transport Panel button in the upper-right corner of the Transport Panel.

The Main Mixer Area

Let's have a closer look at the Main Mixer of the Record interface. Before you begin, press the F5 key on your computer keyboard to maximize this area.

The Main Mixer is divided into three areas:

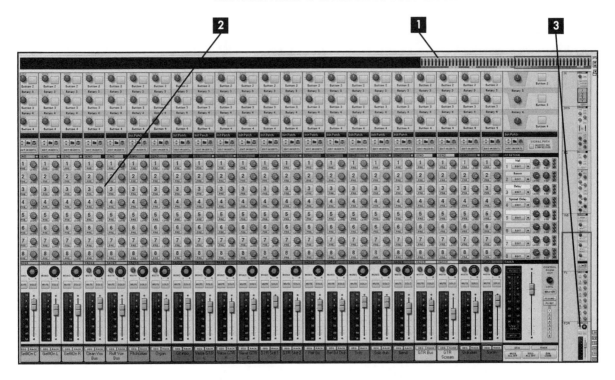

1 Mixer Navigator—Located just above the Main Mixer, this is used to scroll left to right through the mixer channels by clicking and dragging on the blue box. You can also click on any area of the Mixer Navigator to jump to that section of the mixer. Once you have made a selection, you'll see the corresponding mixer channels below.

2 Main Mixer—This is where you make changes to a channel strip's volume, panning, and effects, such as EQ and Dynamics.

3 Channel Strip Navigator—Located at the far right of the Main Mixer area, this is used to scroll up and down the channel strips of the Main Mixer. This can be done by clicking and dragging up or down on the blue box.

The Channel Strip

Looking at the Main Mixer, you'll see that it is composed of several identical components on the mixer called *channels*. Each of these channels corresponds to a rack device and sequencer track, which you'll explore in a couple of pages. When you view these channels vertically, you're viewing what's known as the *channel strip*. Each of these strips has identical features. As the channel strip runs vertically, you can use the Channel Strip Navigator to click and drag up or down to view its various points of interest.

1 Input—This is used to set the volume of the instrument or voice you're going to record.

2 Signal Path—Use this to alter the way the audio will flow through the strip. By default, this is set to Dyn > EQ > Insert, which means the audio will flow from the dynamics to the equalizer to the insert point.

3 Dynamics—Use this to introduce a compressor and/or noise gate to your audio.

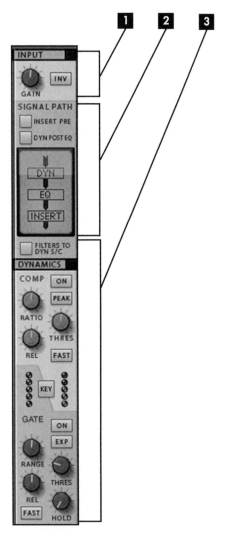

Now click and drag the Channel Strip Navigator down slightly in order to view the next group of channel strip components.

1. EQ—Use this to introduce equalization to your audio.

2. Inserts—Use this to insert effects, such as filters, distortions, chorus, and more, to your audio.

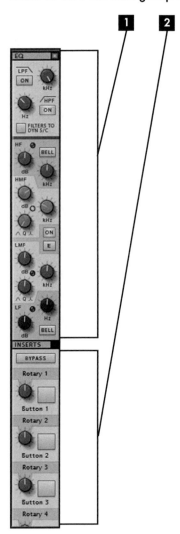

Now click and drag the Channel Strip Navigator down one more time to view its final components.

1 FX Send—Use this area to introduce send effects, such as reverb and delay, to your audio.

2 Fader—Use this to adjust the volume of your audio as it passes through the previous sections. You can solo, mute, and pan your audio as well.

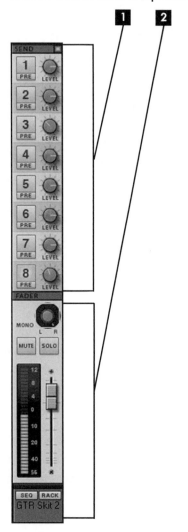

By the way, if you want to simplify the way you look at the channel strip, you can always use the Show/Hide buttons located in the lower-right corner of the Channel Strip Navigator.

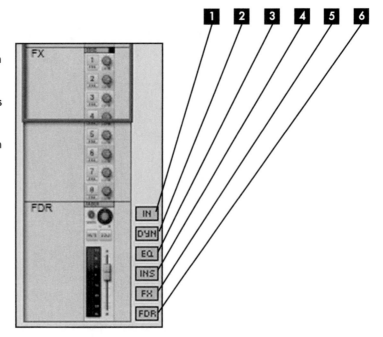

1 IN—Show/hide the Input section of the channel strip.

2 DYN—Show/hide the Dynamics section of the channel strip.

3 EQ—Show/hide the EQ section of the channel strip.

4 INS—Show/hide the Insert section of the channel strip.

5 FX—Show/hide the FX section of the channel strip.

6 FDR—Show/hide the Fader section of the channel strip.

At the bottom of every channel strip are a couple of buttons to allow you to see your channel in the Record Sequencer (SEQ) of the Rack (RACK). Before continuing to the next section, select any channel in the Main Mixer and click on the Rack button.

The Rack

The Record Rack is where all of the creating, routing, and editing happens for your virtual instruments, audio tracks, and effects (called *devices*) in a Record song. The devices within the Rack are displayed in a series of columns that can be navigated either by using the arrow keys on your keyboard, the scroll wheel on your mouse, or by using the Rack Navigator to the far right of the Rack. Also note that you can fold or unfold any device in the Rack by clicking on the triangle button located in the upper-left corner of each device.

You can make the Rack as simple or as complicated as you like, so let's look at this in its most basic form. Trust me—you'll have plenty of time to really dig into this later. From the File menu, select File > New From Template > Song Starter.

Once the new song opens, press the F6 key on your computer keyboard to maximize the Rack area. Let's take a quick look at what's in the Rack:

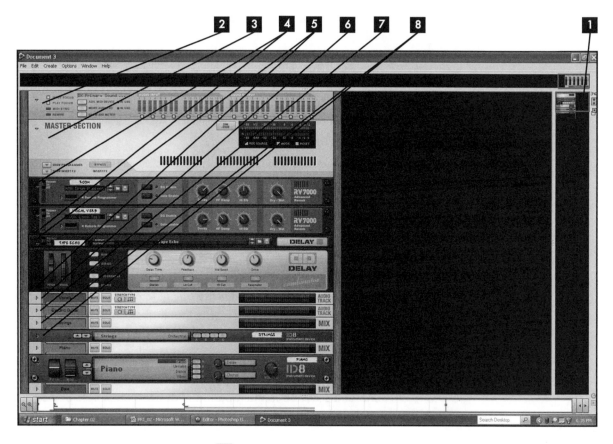

1 Rack Navigator—Use this to view any Rack device by clicking and dragging up and down or, when there are several devices in a song, left to right.

2 Hardware Device—Use this to route your audio in and out of Record. This device has the ability to send and receive 64 separate channels of audio.

3 Master Section—Use this to set up the master effects for your song, such as adding some compression or equalization.

4 RV7000 Advanced Reverb—This is an effect device used to introduce a reverberation effect to your mix. Note that there are two instances of them loaded up in this song.

5 Delay—This is an effect device used to introduce a delay effect to your mix.

6 Audio Track 1—Use this device to set up your audio for recording. From here you can assign an input source, add insert effects, and apply time stretching. This track has a vocal recorded onto it.

7 Audio Track 2—This device is identical to Audio Track 1, except this track has a guitar recorded on it.

8 Mix—This device is used to route virtual instruments to your Record song. In this case, the Mix has been loaded with the ID8 virtual instrument, which is loaded with the Strings patch. Note that there are three additional Mix devices below it, which are loaded with Piano, Bass, and Drum patches.

The Back of the Rack

Another fun feature of Record is the ability to route audio and devices as you please, and in a way that makes sense to anyone who's worked in a studio with a patch bay. If anything, it sure looks cool when someone is looking over your shoulder.

Press the Tab key on your computer keyboard to swing the Rack around and scroll up to the top of the Rack for this simple demonstration.

1 **Navigate** your mouse to the **Audio Out section** of the Hardware Device.

2 **Locate output 1**, which should have a cable attached to it from the left output of the Master Section.

3 **Click and drag** the **cable** to output 3 until it turns to a red color and release your mouse. The left output of the Master Section should now be connected to output 3 on the Hardware Device.

The Sequencer

The Sequencer is the compositional tool of any DAW software, and the Record Sequencer is chock full of powerful tools and features to meet the needs of any digital musician, both old and new. Within the Sequencer, you'll be able to record your audio, or sequence your virtual instruments in no time.

Very briefly, a sequencer displays its audio and MIDI data in a linear view, which simply means that the information is read from left to right. A song will start at the far left of a sequencer, and will slowly progress to the right as the song plays through. You can view where you are in the song by following the position indicator, which scrolls along the timeline.

Before proceeding, press the F7 key on your computer keyboard to maximize the Sequencer. The Record Sequencer is split up into six different areas:

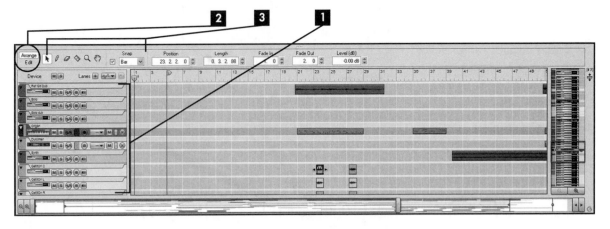

1 **Track List**—This is where all of the separate tracks of your song are listed vertically.

2 **Arrange/Edit Mode**—Use this to toggle between the Arrange and Edit modes of a selected sequencer track.

3 **Toolbar**—Use this to edit your sequencer tracks with basic tools, such as cut, copy, and paste.

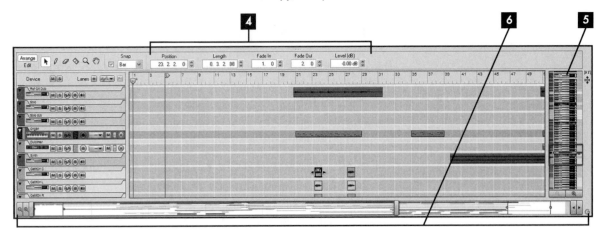

4 **Inspector**—Use this to display where you are in a song, as well as your levels and fade points.

5 Track Navigator—Use this to scroll through your Track list.

6 Song Navigator—Use this to scroll through the timeline of your song.

The Transport Panel

While the Sequencer can be thought of as the composition tool, the Transport Panel can be thought of as its vital counterpart. This is what drives the Record Sequencer. There are a lot of buttons on the Transport that should look familiar to you, so it's actually very easy to get acquainted with.

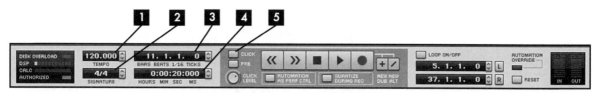

1 Tempo—Use this to change the speed of your song. You can either click and drag up and down in the Tempo dialog or simply use the spin controls.

2 Signature—Use this to change the time signature of your song. You can click and drag up and down in the Signature dialog or simply use the spin controls.

3 Song Position—Use this to jump to a specific part of your song in Bars/Beats/16th notes/Ticks.

4 Time Position—Use this to jump to a specific part of your song in Hours/Minutes/Seconds/Milliseconds.

5 Click—Use this button to turn off and on your click track, which is your metronome.

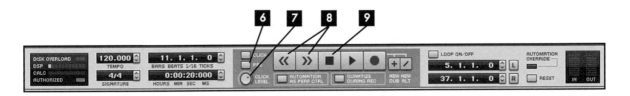

6 Pre—Use this button to create a click track pre-count before you begin recording.

7 Click Level—Use this to adjust the volume of your click track.

8 Rewind/Fast-Forward—Use these buttons to rewind or fast-forward through your song.

9 Stop—Use this button to stop your song. Click it two times to jump to the beginning of your song.

10 Play/Record—Use these to play your song and record new tracks, respectively.

11 Automation as Perf Control—Use this to record parameter automation in your song.

12 Quantize During Recording—Use this to automatically adjust the timing of your virtual instrument tracks via MIDI as you record them.

13 New Dub—Use this to record additional notes over notes that have been previously recorded.

14 New Alt—Use this to record alternative notes over notes that have been previously recorded.

15 Loop—Use this to turn the loop function on or off.

16 Loop Points—Use these to set the beginning (left) of your loop and the end (right) of your loop.

17 L/R—Use these buttons to jump to the left and right loop points.

18 Automation Override Reset—Use this to record new automation data over previously recorded automation data.

19 Audio Input/Output Meters—Use these to measure your audio input and output signals.

If you're wondering about the indicators on the far left of the Transport Panel, they simply indicate how much of your computer's CPU you are using, and whether your computer is authorized to use Record or not.

As you can see, learning the layout of Record is really not that difficult. It's just a matter of understanding the basic tools and functions. Now, let's push on so you can record your first audio track.

3 } Recording Your First Track

In this chapter, I'm going to take you through setting up your first song in Record and show you how easy it is to record your first audio track in the program. As you progress through the rest of this book, you'll take what you learn here and build on it; this should give you a really solid foundation upon which to complete your first song.

Please note that you can go through this entire chapter with Record running in Demo mode or either of the two types of authorization (Ignition Key or Web Authorization). However, while you can save your song in Demo mode, you will not be able to reopen your song without the Ignition Key or Web Authorization.

Creating Your First Audio Track

Let's start by first launching Record, which should bring up the default Record song. This song is pretty much empty with the exception of a few effects that are loaded up and ready to use. Once the song is open, you can create your first audio track. Navigate to the Create menu and select Create Audio Track. An audio track should now be created.

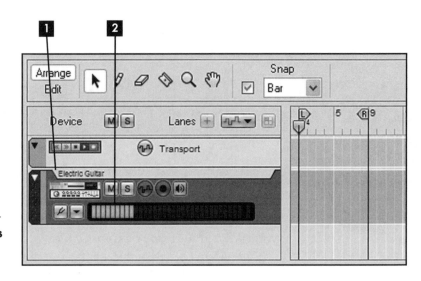

1 **Double-click** on the **name** of the track and name it whatever you want. In this example, I've named it Electric Guitar.

2 At this point, you can plug your instrument into the first audio input on your audio interface. You should immediately start **seeing audio levels** on the **Input Peak meter**. You should also hear your audio playing back through your speakers or headphones.

Let's say you've gone through these steps, and you're not seeing or hearing anything. Here are a couple of quick possibilities.

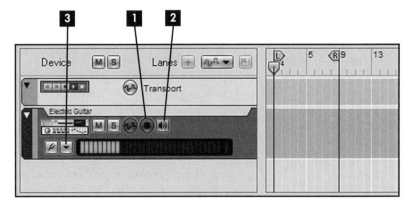

1 Make sure that the **Record Enable button** is **active**. If not, click on it, and you should hear audio.

2 Make sure that the **Enable Monitoring for Track button** is **active**. If not, click on it, and you should hear audio.

3 Make sure that you have **selected** the **correct input** on your audio interface. Click on the Select Audio Input arrow and select the appropriate input.

If none of these suggestions help, refer back to Chapter 1 to make sure you have your audio card properly set up.

Tune It Up

If you're a guitar player, the one thing you constantly have to do (aside from avoiding the urge to buy more gear) is keep your instruments in tune. As luck would have it, Record includes a tuner for every track, so you can keep your guitar, bass, or other stringed instrument in tune and ready to record.

1 Click on the **Enable Tuner button**.

2 The **Input Peak meter** should now become the **tuner**. Play a note on your stringed instrument, and you should see the name of the note that's being played and an indicator to tell you if the note is in tune or not.

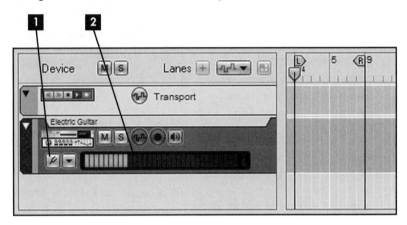

Play through all of the notes and get your instrument in tune. When you are done, click on the Enable Tuner button again, and the audio track will switch back to the Input Peak meter.

Get a Rockin' Sound

At this point, you're almost ready to start recording. However, the rocker inside of me needs to set the mood before recording. No, I'm not talking about turning the lights down low and burning a little incense to set the mood. (Actually, that's not a half-bad idea.) What I am talking about is finding "the sound" before you start recording. Setting the right levels and enhancing the tone is the name of the game here, and this holds true for any instrument you plan to record. If you record instruments with a bland uninspired sound, that's the sound you'll be fighting against as you mix and master your song later. The better way to go is to set up a good, solid rock guitar sound so that the recording can be the best it can be.

Let's start this tutorial by pressing the F6 key on your computer keyboard to maximize the Rack.

1 Go to the Create menu and select Line 6 Guitar Amp. This will **create** an instance of the **Line 6 Guitar Amp** effect.

2 Play a note on your guitar, and you should **hear** the **audio** going through the Line 6 Guitar Amp effect, which by default is set to the Brit Drive preset.

Not happy with the sound, you say? Not a problem; you have 24 different presets to play with, plus you can create additional presets.

Here's how to change the presets.

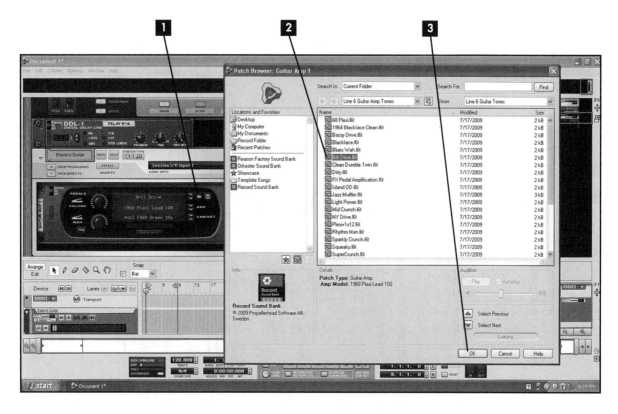

1 **Click** on the **Browse Patch button** on the Line 6 interface. This will launch the Patch Browser window. By default, all of the available patches for the Line 6 amp are listed in the Patch Browser.

2 **Highlight** a **patch** to preview it, and then play a note on your guitar to hear the effect. You can continue to select patches to preview them until you find one you like.

3 Once you've found the one you're happy with, **click** on the **OK button** to load it into the Line 6 Guitar Amp.

When you're done, make sure to press the F6 key again.

Would Ya Like a Little 'Verb with That?

Personally, I think a great guitar tone is incomplete without some reverb (echo) to go along with it. And as luck would have it, the default Record song has a couple of reverbs already loaded up. You just need to access the effect by using the Main Mixer. Press the F5 key on your computer keyboard to begin.

1️⃣ Click and drag the Channel Strip Navigator down to the FX section.

2️⃣ Looking at the Main Mixer, you have eight different send effects and returns. The first two sends and returns are the reverbs. Click on the FX1 Send button to activate it. The button should turn blue.

3️⃣ If you play a note on your guitar, you will hear the Line 6 Guitar Amp and a lot of reverberation. Adjust the Level knob on FX1 send to increase or decrease the effect.

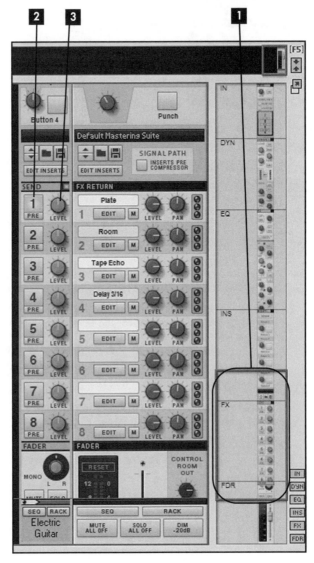

When you're done, make sure to press the F5 key again.

Tempo and Click

The last thing to set up is the tempo of your song and the click track to help keep you in time.

1 Double-click on the Tempo field and **type** in your **tempo**. Personally, I like to start around 100 BPM, as it's a tempo nearly anyone can play comfortably. Press Enter on your computer keyboard, and you're set.

Now let's set the click track.

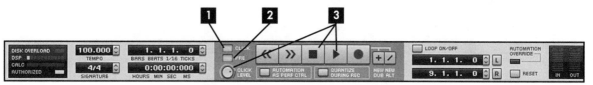

1 **Click** on the **Click button** to activate the click track. Also note that you can use the C key on your computer to do the same thing.

2 **Click** on the **Pre button** to activate the precount. This will give you one full measure of clicks before Record starts recording. It's a good way to set yourself up for recording a decent take.

3 **Click** on the **Play button** in the Transport Panel to start the Sequencer, and then use the Click Level knob to adjust the volume of the click track. When you're done, click on the Stop button twice to send the position indicator back to the beginning of the song.

One, Two, Three, Four... RECORD!

All right, it's finally time to record your first track. For this exercise, you should use your computer keyboard so that you don't waste time going back and forth from your mouse to your instrument.

Get ready, take a deep breath, and let's record a track.

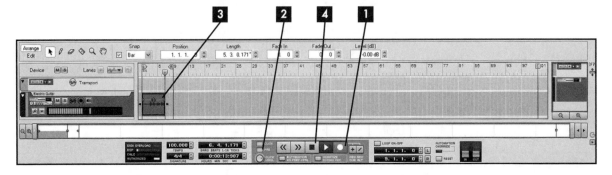

1 Click on the **Record button** in the Transport Panel to start the Sequencer. You can also press the asterisk (*) key on your keyboard.

2 Assuming that the **Pre button** is **active**, you'll get a one bar count off and then the Sequencer will begin to record.

3 **Start playing**. If this is your first recording in this program, don't worry about timing. This is just for demonstration.

4 When you're done recording, **click** on the **Stop button** in the Transport Panel or just press the spacebar on your computer keyboard.

Personalize and Save Your Record Song

When it comes to using a computer to compose and record your songs, you can never save your song enough. You never know when you might experience a power outage, or even a computer crash. Believe me, I could tell you some stories.

Before you do this though, let's take a minute to personalize your song. Select File > Song Information.

1 Fill in the **Text in Window Title field**. This will appear next to the song's name in the upper-left corner of your screen the next time you load the song.

2 The **More Information field** is used to **add any other relevant information**. Who played on the song? What were you thinking when you wrote the song? Copyright information. You get the picture.

3 The **Song Splash area** is used to **insert a picture** of you, or the band, or the album cover. It must be a JPEG file and not exceed 256x256 pixels. If you check the Show Splash on Song Open box, the JPEG file will show up when you load the song.

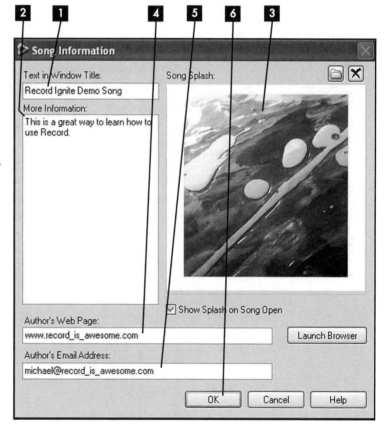

4 The **Author's Web Page field** is for you to **reference** your personal or band **website**. (Is there anyone who doesn't have a Facebook or MySpace page these days?)

5 The **Author's Email Address field** is for you to **input your email address**. Be careful though—you may get your Inbox overloaded with fan mail.

6 Click OK.

Like all DAW programs, Record can save your song by simply selecting File > Save. What's unique in the way that Record saves a song is that the song file will include all of the audio and MIDI as embedded data. Normally when you save a song in most other DAW apps, the audio will be stored in a separate folder, which can get a little complicated when you want to take your song to another computer. But the way that Record does it is quite unique, as the song file is an all-in-one solution.

Record also offers a unique method for saving your completed song, called Save and Optimize. This function optimizes your over-all song. For example, if you record a guitar track but find that you either want to remove parts of the audio track, or the entire track all together, the process can leave data fragments in the Record song. This is similar to the idea of a fragmented hard drive, which all computer geeks know (come on, you know who you are) is a bad thing when it comes to storing data. Disk fragments can cause inconsistencies, and possibly file corruption, so the Save and Optimize feature is a good tool to utilize.

At this point, you can now select Save and Optimize from the File menu. Record will copy the actively used audio files within your song and resave them all into your Record song file. But there are a couple of things to remember. First, this process may take a few minutes to finish, so don't worry if it seems like it's taking a long time. Second, the newly optimized song file might be a little smaller than the original, as the fragmented audio bits have been removed and optimized.

Congratulations! You've just made and saved your first recording! At this point, you can turn off the click track and press the Play button to hear your recording. Don't forget to save your song.

In the next chapter, I'll show you some basic editing techniques.

4 } Basic Editing with Record

Once you have recorded the basic tracks of your new hit single, you might find yourself second guessing your work while listening to it play back. You might catch yourself thinking, "The timing on that guitar part was a little late," or "That vocal take was a little too loud." This is all part of the creative process of recording your songs where you'll find yourself switching from the musician to the producer. At this point, you'll now want to start performing alterations, or edits, to your song. In this chapter, I'll take you through some very basic edits that you can do to the recorded parts within your song. You'll see some more advanced edits in Chapter 6.

Clip-Based Edits

Every edit that you'll be making in this chapter revolves around the term clip. This term is used to describe a part created in Record that contains data, such as an audio recording. If you'll recall from the previous chapter, you created your first audio recording. That recording would now be called a clip. Once these clips have been created, they can be edited in a variety of ways. You can move them, copy them, create simple volume and panning adjustments, and so on. I'll refer to this as *clip-based editing*.

The best thing about clip-based editing is that it is all *non-destructive* editing, which means that you can always undo any edits you've made to your clips. Believe me—it comes in handy in a big way.

Resizing Your Clip

The first edit you're going to do is shorten, or *resize*, a clip. This is very useful when you have a lot of empty space at the beginning or end of a clip. Make sure your mouse is set to the Selector tool (use the Q key on your computer keyboard to select it).

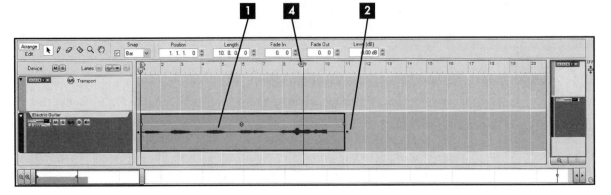

1 **Navigate** your mouse to the **clip you created** in the previous chapter and click on it once to select it.

2 Once it is selected, **navigate** your mouse to the **end of the clip**. You'll see an arrow icon pointing to the right. This is called the Clip Resize handle.

3 **Click and drag** the **Clip Resize handle** to the left to start resizing the clip.

4 When you get to Bar 9 on the Sequencer timeline, **release** the **mouse**.

Fine-Tuning a Resize with Snap

The Snap function of Record makes it possible to make either very precise or broad resizes to your clips. By default, the Snap value is set to Bar, which means that when you make any sort of edit to a clip, whether it's a resize or otherwise, it will be made in increments of bars. If you set this to a finer value, such as 8th notes, the edits will be made in 8th-note increments. Let's have a quick look at this.

Before beginning this exercise, make sure that Snap is active by using the S key on your computer keyboard or by clicking on the check box next to the Snap drop-down menu.

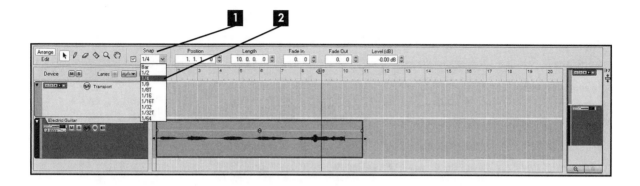

1 **Navigate** your mouse to the **Snap pull-down menu**, and then click on it to display all of the different note values.

2 **Select** the **quarter note (1/4) value.**

Select your clip again and make an adjustment to the Clip Resize handle by clicking and dragging it to the left or right. The clip edits should now be much finer than in the previous exercise.

Copy and Paste

Another popular clip-based edit is copying and pasting your clips. This works exactly like a word processor, except you're copying and pasting music, not words. There are two ways to copy and paste your clips. The first way is by using the Edit menu.

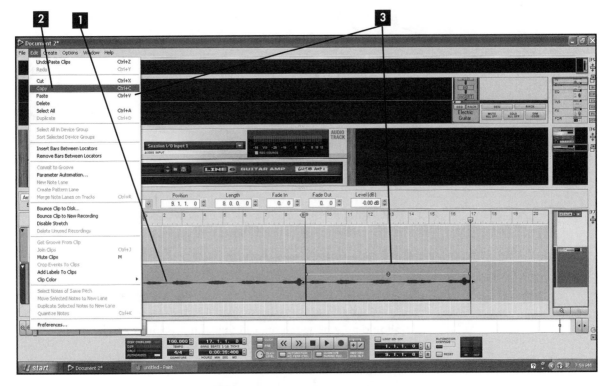

1 **Navigate** your mouse to **your clip** of audio and click on it once to select it.

2 **Navigate** to the Edit menu and **select Copy** (or press Ctrl+C).

3 Now **select Paste** from the Edit menu (or press Ctrl+V). This will place a copy of the clip at the end of the original clip.

You can also copy and paste your clips with the mouse and the Ctrl key on your computer keyboard.

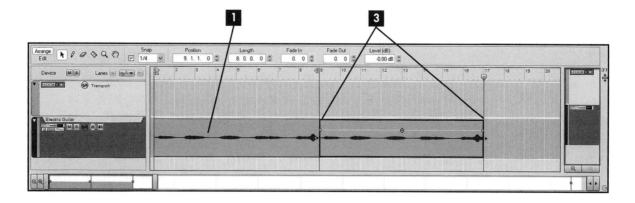

1 Click on the **clip** to select it, and then hold down the Ctrl key on your computer keyboard.

2 Click and drag the **clip** with your mouse while holding down the Ctrl key. This will create a copy of the clip with a little plus icon (+) just below the selector.

3 Once you have found a position in your song to place your copy, **release the mouse** button.

You can also use this method to copy and paste several clips from different tracks, and I'll show you how to do that in Chapter 6.

Levels and Fades

Along with moving and copying clips in Record, you can also alter the levels and fades for an individual clip. This gives you meticulous control over the basic mix of your song.

Changing Clip Levels

Let's first have a go at changing the level on a clip.

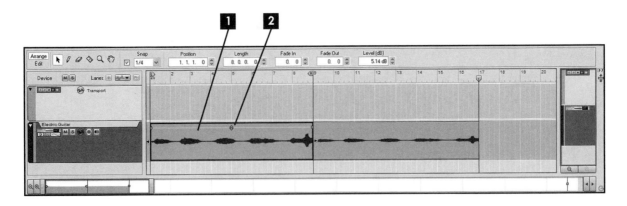

1 **Select** your **clip** by clicking on it with your mouse.

2 **Click and drag** up or down on the **Clip Level handle** to change the level of the clip. Notice that as you do this, the waveform displayed within the clip grows and shrinks.

Changing Clip Fades

Changing clip fades is a fantastic tool to have at your disposal when mixing your song. Let's say you have a guitar part that needs a fade in at the beginning for a guitar solo. You can place a fade in of any length at the start of a clip, and you can create a fade out at the end. This helps to keep the mix punchy and the song a bit more creative.

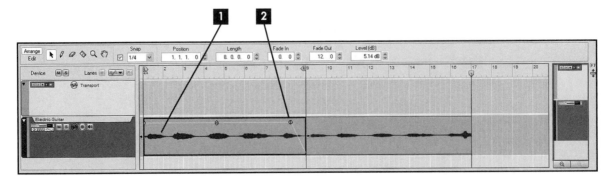

1 **Select** your **clip** by clicking on it with the mouse.

2 **Click and drag** right or left to the **Clip Fade handles** to create a fade in or fade out. Notice that as you do this, the waveform displayed within the clip changes accordingly.

Note that you can make much more precise adjustments to the fades on a clip when you turn off Snap, which can be done by pressing the S key on your computer keyboard.

In Chapter 6, I'll show you how to set up a crossfade, which allows you to fade out one clip while another fades in simultaneously.

Split, Mute, and Join Clips

The final clip-based edits I'll discuss in this chapter are Split, Mute, and Join. These edits allow for some interesting possibilities when editing your Record song.

Splitting Clips

Splitting clips in Record is a great feature, as it allows you to literally cut out the parts of a song you may not want to use and just delete them. You might also want to simply split a clip and use that clip at a different point in your song. Before beginning, make sure that Snap is activated by using the S key on your computer keyboard and that it's set to Bar.

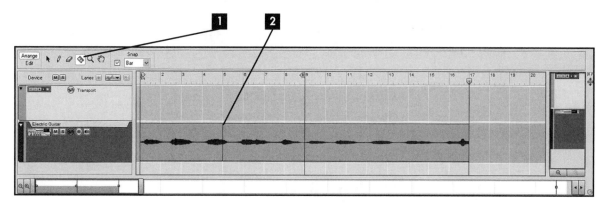

1 **Select** the **Razor tool** from the Sequencer toolbar. Also note that you can press the R key on your computer keyboard.

2 **Navigate** your mouse to a **clip of audio** in your Record song and click on it anywhere with the Razor tool. This should split the clip at the nearest bar in the Sequencer timeline.

Once you have split your clip, you can cut any unwanted clips of data by doing the following exercise. Make sure that you have chosen the Selector tool from the Sequencer toolbar before you begin.

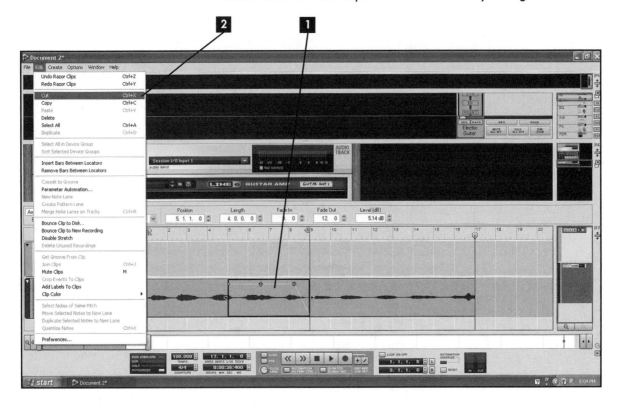

1 **Select** any **clip** by clicking on it.

2 **Select Cut** from the Edit menu. The clip will be erased. (You can also use the Backspace or Delete key on your computer keyboard.)

Muting Clips

Muting clips is probably one of the easiest edits to perform in Record, as you only need to use the M key on your computer keyboard. This edit really comes in handy when you want to mute a specific part in a song, like a vocal take that doesn't seem to fit or a guitar solo that was played too long. You can also use this musically to create tempo-based mute patterns for guitars and drum loops.

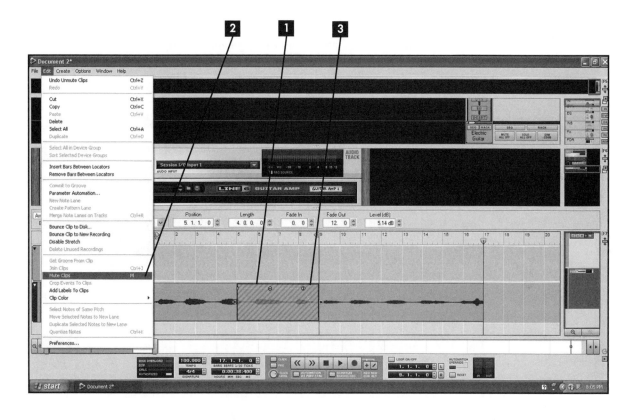

1 **Select** any **clip** in your Record song by clicking on it with the Selector tool.

2 **Select Mute Clips** from the Edit menu or press the M key on your computer keyboard.

3 Have a look at the muted clip, and you'll see that it's now grayed out with diagonal lines marked throughout.

Joining Clips

If you have a lot of erased clips on a track in your Record song, you can use the Join Clips function to group them together to create a brand new clip. Throughout the creative process of writing and recording your songs in Record, you will no doubt create a lot of audio clips on a single track. In my case, I tend to record a lot of pick up guitar parts at the beginning and end of verses, and this creates additional clips on my guitar tracks. This can lead to a lot of additional clutter in my Arrange window. By using the Join Clips function, I can merge all of that clutter into a single, linear clip.

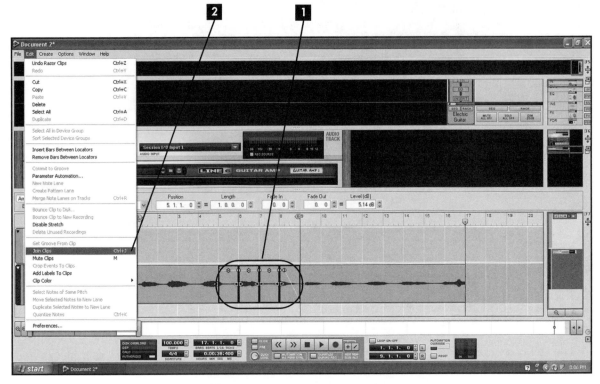

1 **Select** a **group of clips** by clicking and dragging a marquee around them with your mouse. Release the mouse and all of the clips should now be selected.

2 **Navigate** to the **Edit menu** and select Join Clips (or press Ctrl+J on your computer keyboard). You should now see a newly created clip.

Throughout this chapter, I've shown you the basic editing tools you'll need in order to tap into the potential of Record. Just remember that, as with learning an instrument, you need to practice using these tools as much as possible to get the hang of them. Once you do this, you'll be able to edit audio in your sleep.

5 } Using MIDI with Record

In this chapter, I'll introduce you to using MIDI with Record. MIDI, or Musical Instrument Digital Interface, is at its simplest a language or code that allows a program like Record to communicate with other devices, such as drum machines, synthesizers, and effects. In the case of Record, MIDI is used to communicate with the soft synth that's provided with the program. The idea here is to provide you with a versatile selection of sounds without a lot of complication.

Before beginning this chapter, make sure that your MIDI keyboard is set up properly. (Refer back to Chapter 1 to review.)

Meet the ID8

The ID8 is Record's one and only soft synth that comes with the program. It is a powerful little synth that offers 36 different sounds, or "patches," that are divided into nine different categories:

- Pianos
- Electric Pianos
- Organs
- Guitars
- Bass
- Strings
- Brass/Woodwinds
- Synths
- Drums/Percussion

Before beginning, create an instance of the ID8 by selecting it from the Create menu. The interface itself is pretty straightforward. Take a minute to familiarize yourself with the layout.

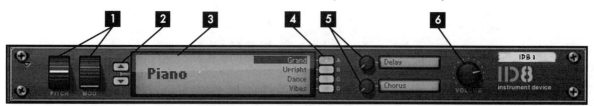

1 The Pitch and Mod wheels are used to change the pitch by bending the pitch up and down, while the modulation will create a wavering or vibrato effect on your loaded patches.

2 The Category up/down buttons are used to select the different patch categories.

3 The Category dialog displays the category. You can click on this to change categories instead of using the up/down buttons to the left. You can also use this to browse instruments, which you'll explore later in this chapter.

4 The Sound Select buttons are used to select the different patches within a category.

5 The Parameter knobs are used to alter specific parameters of each patch. The parameters have been preselected for you and will change from patch to patch.

6 The Volume knob is used to change the volume of the ID8.

Recording Your First MIDI Track

Now that you've been introduced to the ID8, it's time to record your first MIDI track. Before beginning, let's make sure everything is ready to go.

1 **Set** the **tempo** to one that is comfortable for you to play at. Remember, the tempo can always be changed later, so don't feel locked into a single tempo.

2 **Click** on the **Click and Precount buttons** to activate them and select a volume for the click.

3 **Click** on the **Loop button** to activate the loop function of the Record Sequencer. When activated, the loop function will cause the position indicator to jump back to the left locator point once it reaches the right locator point. This will enable you to record additional MIDI data onto your ID8 Sequencer track.

Now you'll select a patch to use for your first recording. I typically start with a drum patch, so go ahead and select the Drum category and choose a patch.

Once you have done this, it's best to familiarize yourself with the individual sounds of the patch and where they are located on your MIDI keyboard controller. Take a few minutes and locate the kick and snare sounds.

You're now ready to record your first MIDI track. Click the Record button on the Transport Panel. You'll get a measure precount, and you're off.

Once you are satisfied with your recording, click the Stop button. Press the Play button to hear your recorded MIDI track play back.

Editing Your MIDI Track with Record

At this point, it would be a good idea to take a closer look at what you just recorded, as well as enhance it with some minor edits. Double-click on the recorded part to switch to the Edit mode in the Record Sequencer.

Let's have a look at the layout of the Edit window.

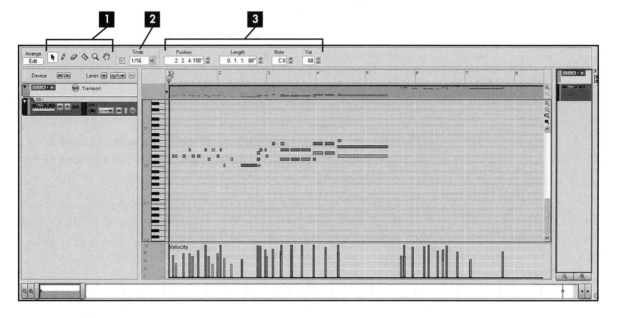

1 The Toolbar contains all of the same tools you've used up till now.

2 Snap is an important part of Edit mode, as you'll see in a few minutes.

3 The Inspector is used as both a display for any selected note, as well as a means to create very intricate edits in your MIDI clips. All selected notes are displayed in the Position, Length, Note, and Velocity fields.

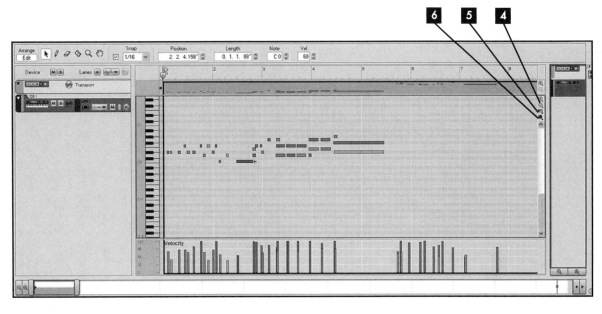

4 The Vertical Zoom tools are used to zoom vertically in and out of your MIDI clips. There are two sets of Zoom tools. One set is used to zoom in and out of the clip, while the other is used to zoom in and out of the actual MIDI notes within the clip.

5 The Note Edit Mode button is used to toggle between the different Edit modes in Record (Key, Drum, and Rex). However, it should be noted that you will probably not need to use these unless you plan to use Reason along with Record. (See the Appendix for more information on Reason.)

6 The Note Lane Performance Parameter Automation button is used to introduce different parameters, such as pitch bend, sustain pedal, and others that can be automated via the Edit mode.

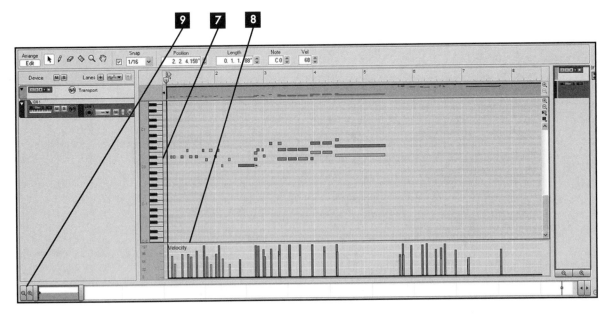

7 The Piano Roll is used to display where the MIDI notes are recorded along the timeline of a selected clip. If you click on any of the key's of the roll, Record will audition any notes that may be loaded on that particular key.

8 The Velocity lane is used to edit the amount of velocity recorded on each MIDI note.

9 The Horizontal Zoom tools are used to zoom horizontally in and out of your MIDI clips.

Moving Individual Notes Around

The first edit you'll look at is moving notes. This is helpful if you either played a wrong note, or if you want to enhance the MIDI recording by introducing some variation.

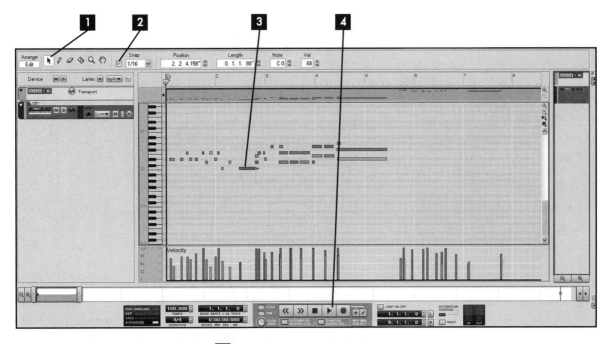

1 **Press** the **Q key** on your computer keyboard to activate the Selection tool.

2 **Activate and set** the **Snap** to 1/16. This will allow you to move the notes by 16th-note increments.

3 **Click** on **any note** and drag it from side to side to change its position. If you click and drag the note up or down, you'll hear the note play back with the new sound assigned to it.

4 **Press Play**, and you should hear the difference in the timing.

Moving a Selection of Notes Around

You can also move a selection of MIDI notes around.

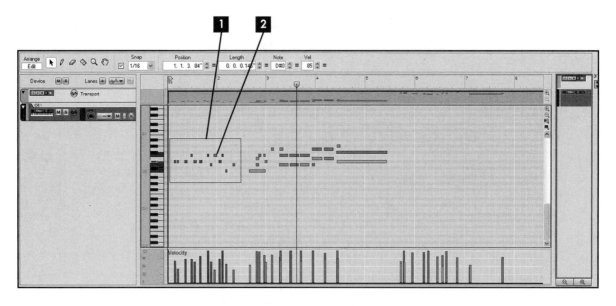

1 With the Selection tool selected, **click and drag** a **marquee**, or a box, around a series of notes to select them.

2 Once the notes have been selected, **click and drag** them **side to side or up and down** to see and hear the results.

Changing Note Lengths

You can also use the Record Sequencer to change the length of an individual note or a group of notes.

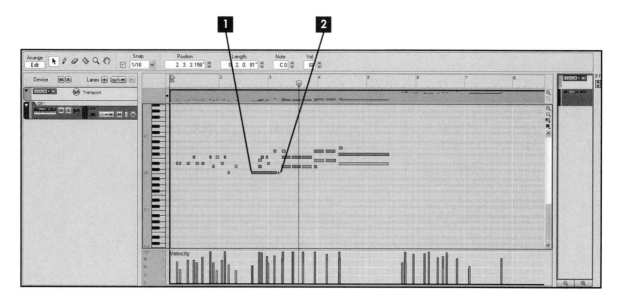

1 Click on a **note** to select it. You will see a handle appear on the right side of the note.

2 Click and drag this **handle** to the right to change the length of the note.

You can also do this to change the length of a group of notes. Select a group of notes, then click and drag on any handle of the selected notes, and they will all change length accordingly.

Drawing and Erasing Notes

If you want to create a MIDI performance for your Record song, but you're not much of a keyboard player, it's not a problem. The Record Sequencer allows you to draw in your MIDI clips note for note, offering you limitless possibilities. Drawing notes is a simple process.

First, you need to select the length of the note you want to draw in. For this example, let's use 8th notes.

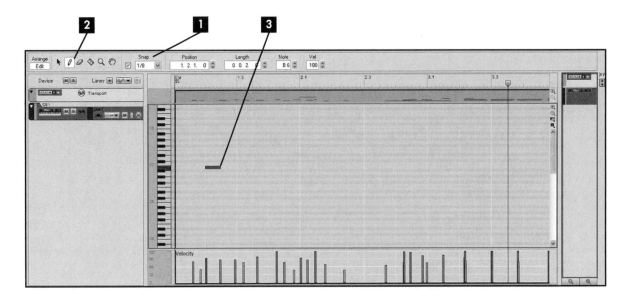

1 Make sure that Snap is active, and then **select 1/8** from the drop-down menu.

2 **Select** the **Pencil tool** by clicking it with your mouse or by pressing the W key on your computer keyboard.

3 Now, **click** anywhere along the **timeline**, and Record will draw in a MIDI note in an 8th-note value.

If you want to erase notes, just follow these steps.

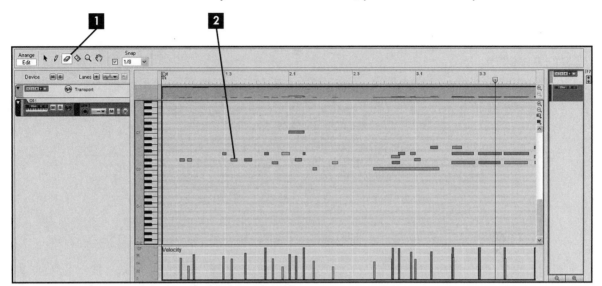

1. **Select** the **Eraser tool** with your mouse or by pressing the E key on your computer keyboard.

2. **Navigate** to a **note** you wish to erase, and click on it. The note will disappear.

If you want to erase a group of notes, click and drag a box around the group of notes with the Eraser tool and release the mouse button. All of the selected notes will be erased.

Editing Velocity

When listening back to your MIDI performance, if you happen to notice a couple of notes or drum hits that sound either a little too loud or soft, this is where editing the velocity or notes can come in handy. *Velocity* is the term used to describe how hard a note is played from your MIDI keyboard. Each MIDI note that is recorded into the Record Sequencer is assigned a velocity. Likewise, every note that is manually written into the Record Sequencer is assigned a velocity. Once recorded, these velocities can be edited by using the Velocity Lane, which is located in the lower portion of the Edit window.

Try the following exercise:

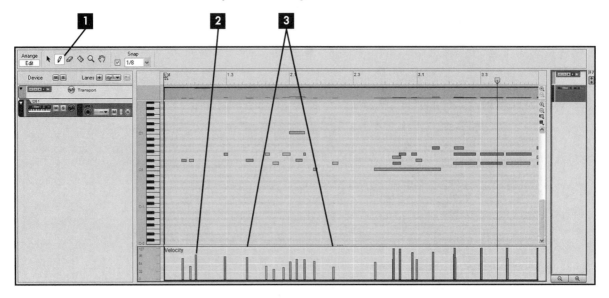

1 Select the **Pencil tool**.

2 **Navigate** to the **velocity of any single note**, and then click above or below it. This will change the velocity of that individual note. Once you do this, you will see that the color of the note and velocity will change accordingly.

3 If you want to edit the velocity of a group of notes, simply **click and drag** across the **velocities of the notes**, and they will change accordingly.

Here's a cool tip. Select a group of notes with the Selector tool, and then select the Pencil tool. Hold down the Shift key, and you can edit the velocities of just the selected notes without affecting the unselected notes.

Using the Tool Window

The Tool Window is a really great feature that was introduced into the Reason program, and it has been faithfully reproduced in Record. The Tool Window is the ultimate shortcut for creating new instances of any Record device, editing MIDI performances, or working with ReGroove.

Navigate your mouse to the Window menu and select Show Tool Window. This will place the Tool Window on the right-hand side of the Record interface. You can also use the F8 key to show and hide the Tool Window at will.

Since this is more of a beginner's book, I'll just focus on some of the easier tools to work with. Select the Tools tab, and let's begin.

Quantize Notes

The Quantize Notes tool is used to correct timing problems. The easiest way to explain it is to think of quantizing as an invisible magnet that pulls and pushes MIDI notes to a determined note value, which is assigned in the Value pull-down menu. Simply select a group of MIDI notes in Edit mode. Once this is done, the Apply button in the Quantize Notes tool will become active. It's extremely easy to use.

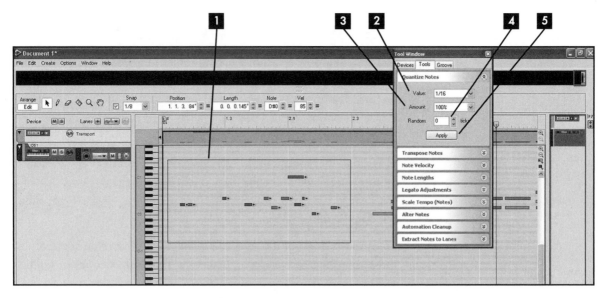

1 Using the Selector tool, **select** a **group of notes** by clicking and dragging a box around them. For the best results, try to find a group of notes that have timing issues.

2 **Assign** a **note value** from the Value pull-down menu. I would suggest values of either 1/8 or 1/16 for your first time out.

3 **Assign** a **quantization amount** by using the Amount pull-down menu.

4 If you want to correct the timing problems but not have the end result sound too robotic, **select** an **amount of ticks** from the Random field.

5 **Click** on the **Apply button**, and Record will quantize the selected MIDI notes.

Here's another cool tip. Select the Quantize During Recording button on the Transport Panel, and Record will automatically quantize your performances as you sequence them in. This is a great feature to use if you are a novice keyboard player or rhythmically challenged. (Don't worry—it happens to the best of us.)

Transpose Notes

The purpose of transposing notes is to change the original pitch of the MIDI notes. Let's say, for example, that you have recorded a MIDI performance in the key of C, but your singer can't sing within that range. With the Transpose Notes tool, you can select a key that your singer can work with.

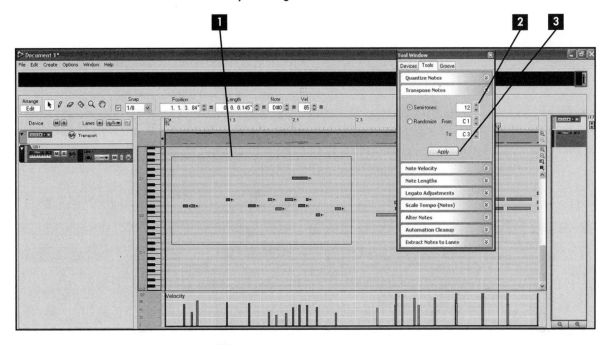

1 **Select a group of MIDI notes.** Using the Selection tool, hold down the mouse and drag a box around the notes.

2 **Use the Semi-tones field** up and down arrows to find a pitch that you want. For example, if you wanted to alter the pitch of your MIDI part by an octave, you would select a value of 12.

3 **Click the Apply button.**

A unique feature of the Transpose Notes tool is the Randomize function.

1 Select a group of MIDI notes.

2 Click on the Randomize option to select it.

3 Set a note range. I suggest using the default settings for this example.

4 Click the Apply button. Record will randomly transpose each note within the range you selected.

Scale Tempo

This tool is one of my favorites, as it allows you to change the tempo of a selected group of MIDI notes. So if you're writing in a drum part, and you need a fast drum fill or if you want to change the overall feeling of your song to a cut time feel, the Scale Tempo might be just what you're looking for.

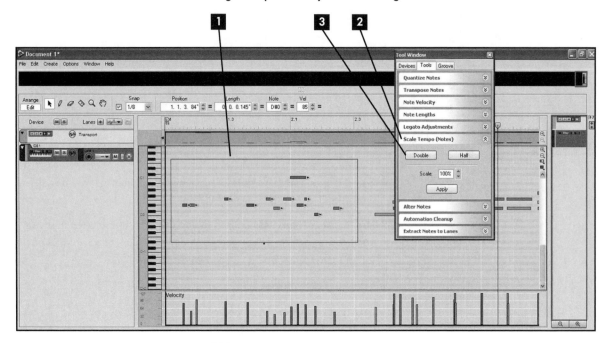

1 Select a group of MIDI notes.

2 Select the Scale Tempo tool.

3 Click on the **Double button** to compress and speed up the tempo of the selected group of notes, or click on the Half button to stretch and slow down the tempo of the selected group of notes. Then click Apply.

You can also use the Scale field of this tool to fine-tune your tempo adjustments to individual notes or a smaller group of notes. The best thing to do here is simply jump in and try different values until you get the results you want.

Getting a Second Monitor

If you feel like the Record interface is getting a little crowded, you would be right. There are a lot of additional tools and windows within Record, not to mention that the Record Rack might also look a little crowded, especially when paired up with the Sequencer and the Main Mixer. Now might be a good time to invest in a second computer monitor for your Record setup. Not only are monitors getting more affordable, but you can also detach the Main Mixer and the Rack to place them on another screen. You can do this by selecting Window > Detach Main Mixer or Window > Detach Rack Window. Doing this will make Record a lot easier to look at, and it should also help you increase your productivity within Record.

As you can see, Record is a powerful MIDI sequencer that rises to the creative challenges of beginning and seasoned users alike. If you find yourself wanting a greater selection of soft synths for your music, Reason would be a great complement to have. (You can learn more about Reason in the Appendix.)

6 ∮ More Editing with Record

In this chapter, I'm going to take you through some of the more advanced editing features of Record. These edits will allow you to take real control of your audio and MIDI performances in your song. Whether you want to write in automation for individual MIDI parameters or piece together different audio clips to create a perfect take, Record can do this and more with ease.

Before beginning this chapter, make sure that you download and open up the Chapter 6 Song from the Cengage Learning website at www.courseptr.com/downloads (and make sure to enter this book's ISBN number).

Inserting and Removing Bars in Your Song

Throughout the recording process, sometimes you'll listen to your song play back and think that it would be great to have a couple of extra bars here or possibly remove some bars there. You might do this if you wanted to record an additional verse or chorus, or possibly introduce a couple of bars of silence between the verse and the chorus for dramatic effect. This is a snap with Record. Try the follow exercise to insert bars into your song.

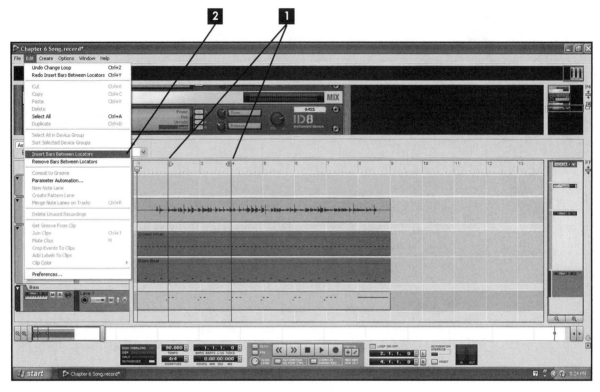

1 First, **set** your **left locator and right locator** at the points that you wish to insert bars into. As you can see, I have set my left locator to bar 2 and the right locator to 4. This will give me two additional bars in my song.

2 **Navigate** to the **Edit menu** and **select Insert Bars Between Locators.**

You should now see the additional bars between your locator points.

To remove bars from a song, just set up the left and right locators as before and select Edit > Remove Bars Between Locators.

Inserting Tempo and Time Changes

Tempo and time changes are one of the best tricks in the book when it comes to making your music more interesting. Record offers a couple of drop-dead easy ways to accomplish this task. This is all done with the Transport Track. Located at the top of the Track list in the Sequencer, the Transport Track governs the overall tempo and time signature of your Record song. With this track, you can simply draw in your tempo and time changes. The tempo and time data that you draw will be displayed on the Track lane, which displays multiple tracks of data contained within a single Sequencer track.

Select the Transport Track, expand it, and try the following exercise.

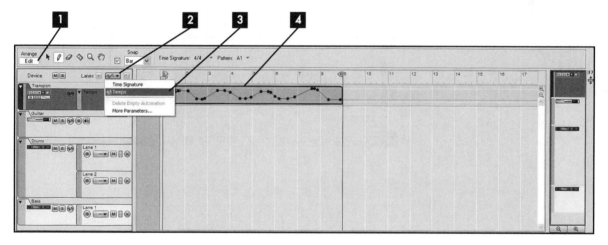

1 Click on the **Edit button** to switch to Edit mode.

2 Click on the **Track Parameter Automation button** in the Sequencer Track list. This will display the available parameters to automate.

3 Select **Tempo**, and a Tempo lane will be created on the Transport Track.

4 Select the Pencil tool, and then **draw** a **Tempo track** by clicking and dragging up and down to the right. Also note that you can hold down the Alt key and the Pencil tool will automatically appear, but you need to continue holding down the Alt key as you draw your edits.

Once you've drawn in a new tempo, press Play to hear the results. Note that these are non-destructive edits. You can always go back to the beginning if you want by selecting Undo from the Edit menu or doing one of the following:

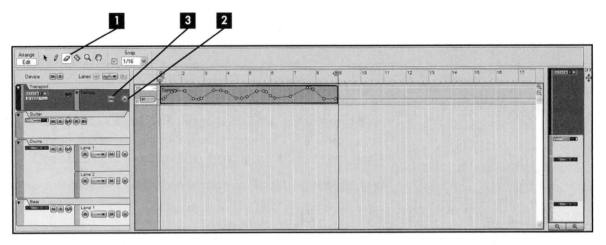

1 Click the **Eraser tool** and simply erase the changes.

2 Delete the automation lane by **clicking** on the **Delete Automation Lane button**.

3 Turn the automation lane off by **clicking** its **power button**.

Now let's have a look at time signature changes. Try the following exercise:

1 **Click** on the **Track Parameter Automation button** in the Sequencer Track list. This will display the available parameters to automate.

2 **Select Time Signature**, and a Time Signature lane will be created on the Transport Sequencer track.

3 You can change the time signature of the entire song by **clicking** on the **Static Value option**, which is set to 4/4 by default. If you click on this, you can select any time signature you want.

4 **Select** the **Pencil tool** and **draw in** a **new time signature** by simply clicking where you'd like the new time signature to start. This will create a new part on the Transport Sequencer track

5 This new part will have a default time signature of 4/4, so just **double-click** on it to **assign a new time signature.** You can also click on the small arrow at the top-left corner of the newly created part and select a new time signature.

At this point, you should probably close the Chapter 6 Song and reopen it, as you have made a lot of changes to the song so far. Reopening the song will allow you to start the next part of this chapter with a clean slate.

Comping Audio Tracks

When I'm recording my tracks, I always try to record multiple takes of the same instrument so I can pick and choose the parts that I would like to compile into a single audio track. This is known as *comping*. Think of it like this: You're recording your vocalist and he or she sings perfectly throughout most of the first half of the song. Then on a second take, the singer isn't really getting the first part of the song down, but they nail it during the second half of the song. Comping allows you to extract the best parts of both takes and create a "perfect take." It may sound a little like cheating, but similar things were done with tape as well back in the analog days of recording.

Assuming that you have closed and reopened the Chapter 6 Song, you'll see an 8-bar audio recording of guitar as well as a couple of MIDI tracks. I recorded three different takes of roughly the same guitar riff in Loop mode. Every time the position indicator would jump back to the left locator, a new take was recorded. Double-click on the recorded clip to open it in Edit mode, then follow these steps.

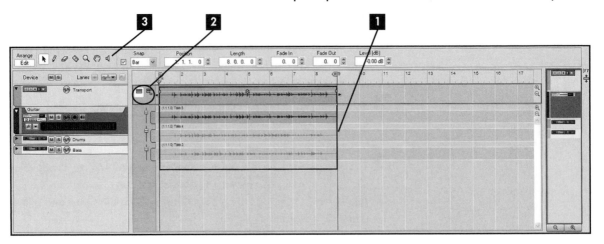

1 All of the different takes of the guitar riff are represented here, each with its own lane.

2 The Single Mode/Comp Mode buttons are used to toggle between the Single mode (on the left) and Comp mode (on the right). With Single mode, only the last recorded take will play back. With Comp mode, every take can play back. Also note that each take has its own volume fader.

3 The Speaker tool is used to audition takes.

At this point, switch to Comp mode, set the Snap value to Bar, and try the following exercise.

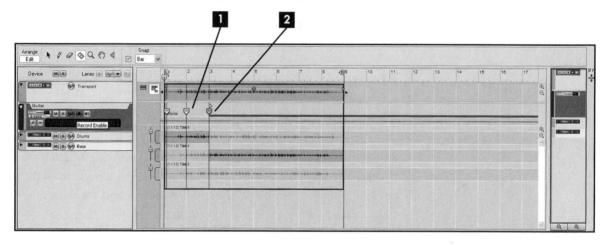

1 Select the Razor tool and **make a cut** at **bar 2** on the Take 5 track. This will create a Cut handle. (Also note that you can hold down the Alt key to make the Razor tool appear, but you will need to continue holding the Alt key as you make changes.)

2 Now **make a cut** at **bar 2** on the Take 4 track. This will create a comp between Take 5 and Take 4.

If you play the song back now, you'll hear a pretty clean transition between Take 5 and Take 4. Now let's get Take 3 into the mix.

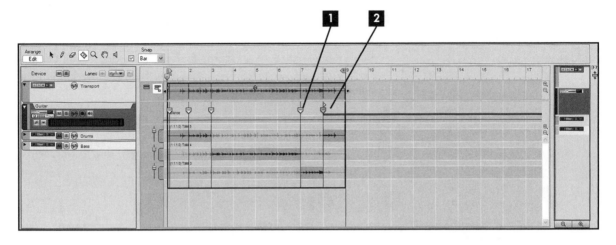

1 With the Razor tool still selected, **make a cut** at **bar 7** on the Take 3 track.

2 Now **make a cut** at **bar 8** on the Take 5 track.

If you listen to the song now, the guitar part is almost perfect. However, there are a couple of pops and clicks you need to clean up. This is easily done by selecting a Cut handle and creating a crossfade by simply clicking and dragging.

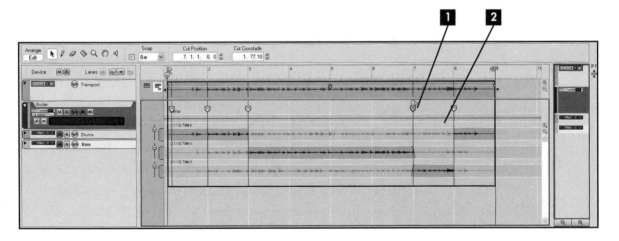

1 With the Selector tool selected, **click** on the **fourth Cut handle**.

2 **Click and drag** just above **the Cut handle** to the right. This will create a crossfade between Take 4 and 3.

You're almost there. Now you just need to clean up the transition between Take 3 and Take 5.

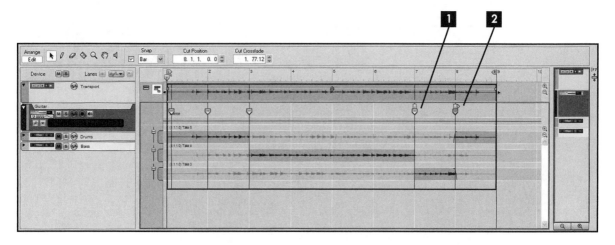

1 With the Selector tool selected, **click** on the **fifth Cut handle**.

2 **Click and drag** just above the **Cut handle** to the right. This will create a crossfade between Take 3 and 5.

Now listen back to the song, and you'll hear a nearly perfect comped guitar track. At this point, you can bounce your comped guitar track down to a single recording. This makes it easier to keep your audio files organized.

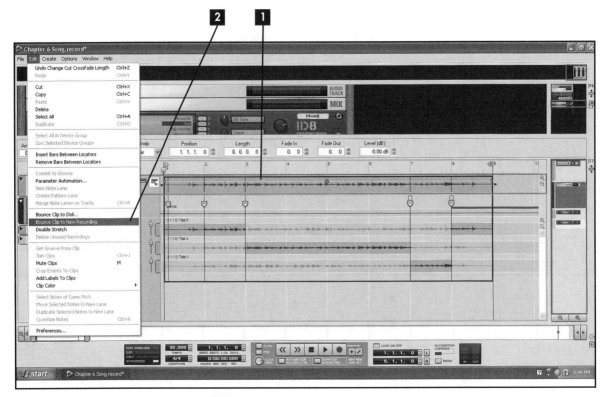

1 Click on the **audio clip** in the Clip Overview area.

2 From the Edit menu, **select Bounce Clip to New Recording**. A new recording will be created, and the guitar track will automatically switch from Comp mode to Single mode.

Before continuing on, make sure to switch back to the Arrange mode.

Automating MIDI Parameters

One of the best features of Record and Reason is its ability to easily automate the individual parameters of the program. I can still to this day remember how difficult a task this was to accomplish back when I started sequencing hardware synths with an Atari music computer. (Yes, I said Atari.) *Automation* is the capability to automatically control equipment by recording its movements. A good example of automation is a hardware mixer with motorized faders that are programmed to automatically move with the mix. Record's automation functions can record the movements of nearly any device parameter, and those movements recur as you play back the song. Additionally, you can manually write in your own automation using the Edit mode of the Record Sequencer.

For this example, you're going to continue using the Chapter 6 Song, as it has a MIDI Bass track going through an instance of the ID8 that needs some automation love. Double-click on the Bass track to view it in Edit mode.

For the following exercise, you're going to write in automation data to the Parameter 1 knob of the ID8 instrument on the Bass track. In this case, Parameter 1 is a tone knob, so writing in automation data will cause the tone to change from a bass-heavy sound to one that's a little more nasal sounding. It's a pretty well-known trick in electronic music.

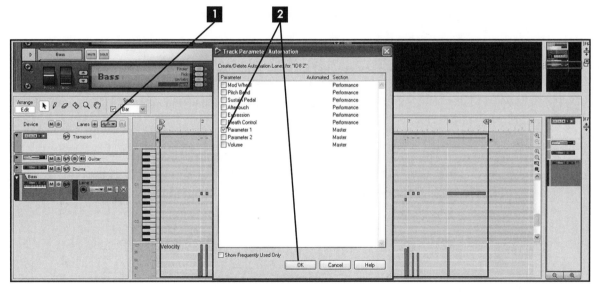

1 Navigate to the **Track Parameter Automation pull-down menu** and **select More Parameters** to open the Track Parameter Automation window. This window is used to select the parameters of the loaded soft synth you wish to automate.

2 **Select Parameter 1** and **click OK**. Note that in this case, Parameter 1 is the Tone knob on the ID8.

At this point, an automation lane has been created on the Bass track of the Record Sequencer.

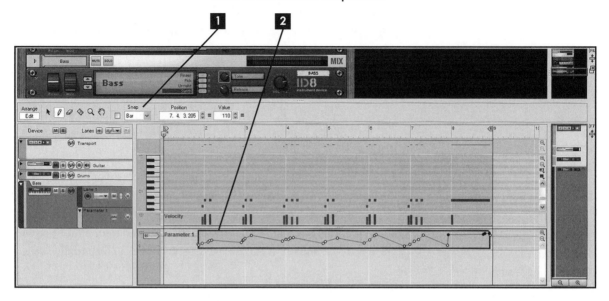

1 Turn off the **Snap function**.

2 Select the Pencil tool and **draw in** an **automation curve** on the Parameter 1 lane of the Bass track. Release the mouse, and the automation curve should be written and automatically cleaned up by the Record Sequencer.

Before moving on, take a minute to notice that there is now a neon green box around the Parameter 1 (Tone) knob of the ID8, which means that there is automation data written to that parameter.

The last automation move to write in here is a pitch bend on the last note of the Bass track. Try the following exercise:

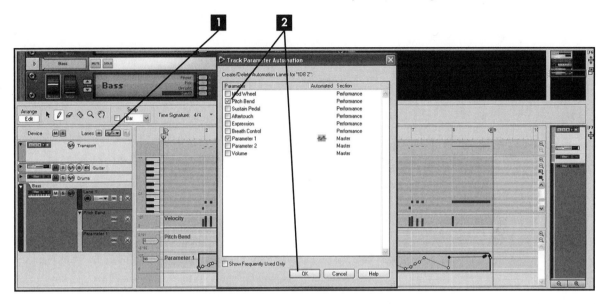

1 Navigate to the **Track Parameter Automation pull-down menu** and **select More Parameters** to open the Track Parameter Automation window.

2 **Select Pitch Bend** and **click OK**. This will create a Pitch Bend automation lane on the Bass track.

Now that the automation lane has been created, you can go ahead and write in the pitch bend.

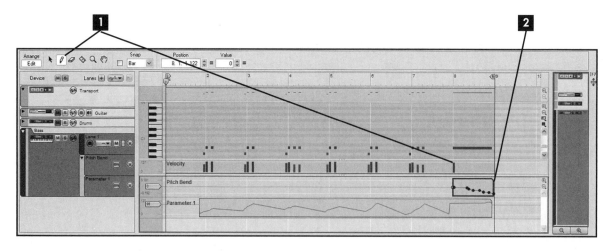

1 **Using** the **Pencil tool,** navigate to the last note and draw in a pitch bend curve.

2 **Release** the **mouse,** and the automation curve should be written and automatically cleaned up by the Record Sequencer.

This is a very basic example of automation, as you're just looking at a couple parameters of a single soft synth. Later on (in Chapter 8), I'll show you how to really put your automation knowledge to work when you mix the Record Demo song.

7 } Using Effects

In Chapter 3, I showed you how to create instances of effects and use them to get a basic sound when you recorded your first audio track. Now that you've gotten a better grip on Record and how it works, let's have a closer look at some of its included effects and how to use them.

When using effects, such as reverbs and delays, it's really easy to go overboard and create space sounds and distorted sonic landscapes. While Record is fully capable of doing that (and I encourage creativity), it's really important to learn the fundamentals of using effects properly. Believe me, there are some mixes I've heard that sound like the music is being played through a washing machine, and while that can be a good sound to use sparingly, it's not so great when the entire record sounds that way. As a listener, you start listening to what's wrong with the mix and lose all focus on the music.

Having said all of this, there's really no wrong way to use an effect in Record, as it offers so many possibilities. However, this chapter should help you grasp the basic understanding of how to use these effects properly.

Send Effects and Insert Effects

There are two ways to use effects in Record, as a send or as an insert. A *send* effect is used to process an assigned portion of a Record track signal. That processed signal is then routed back into the Main Mixer and mixed together with the unprocessed, or "dry," signal. For example, if you have a guitar track and a RV7000 Reverb assigned to send 1 in the Main Mixer, you can use the Send 1 knob to "send" a portion of your dry signal to the RV7000. Once the signal is processed by the RV7000, it is then "returned" to the Record mixer in order to be mixed in with the dry signal on channel 1.

Additionally, you can use the Send 1 knobs on the other mixer channels of the Main Mixer to send additional channels of audio to the same instance of the RV7000 Reverb. This will save you a significant amount of your computer's processing speed.

An *insert* effect is used to process the entire signal of a Record track. For example, if you were to route the outputs of that same guitar track directly to the inputs of a compressor, and then connect those outputs to the inputs of a Record Mixer channel, this would be considered an insert effect.

So, which effects would be considered sends and which would be considered inserts? Well, technically, all of the effects that are included with Record can be used either way, but the effects that have "tail ends" or "reflections of audio" such as the RV7000 reverb or the DDL-1 delay, are prime examples of send effects, while compressors, EQs, and distortions make for good insert effects as those effects can be heard instantaneously.

Creating a Send Effect

Let's take a minute to go through the steps of creating a send effect. Start with a clean slate by selecting File > New. This will create a new blank song; although there are some send effects already set up, you can still use this. Remember, there are eight send effect slots on the Main Mixer.

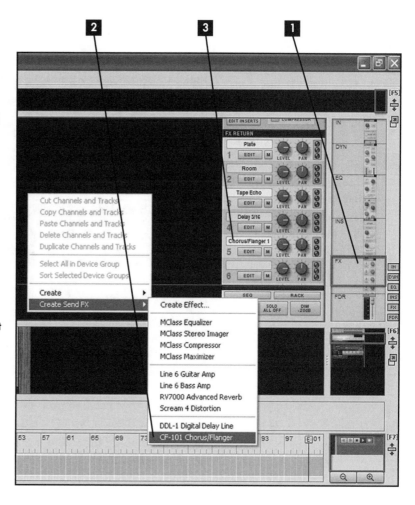

1 Click on the **FX area** in the Channel Strip Navigator to display the FX Return section in the Main Mixer. You should see four effects already loaded up (Plate, Room, Tape Echo, and Delay 3/16).

2 **Right-click** anywhere in the **blank area** of the Main Mixer and select Create Send FX > CF-101 Chorus/Flanger.

3 An **instance** of the **CF-101** should now appear in the fifth slot of the FX Return section of the Main Mixer. This means that the send effect has been created and is ready to be used with send 5 on the Main Mixer.

Creating an Insert Effect

Creating insert effects is easy to accomplish in a few short steps. In order to work with this, you will need an empty audio track. Navigate to the Create menu and select Create > Create Audio Track. This will place an empty audio track device in the Rack and a blank audio track in the Record Sequencer. Press F6 to maximize the Rack and try the following exercise:

1 Navigate to the Audio Track 1 device and **click** on the arrow to expand it, then click on the **Show Insert FX button**. This will show the empty insert rack.

2 Right-click in the insert rack and **select Create > Line 6 Guitar Amp**. This will create an instance of the amp and route itself to the audio track device as an insert effect.

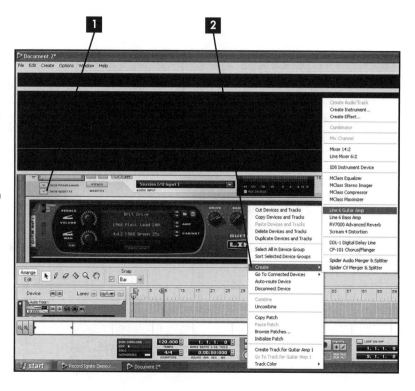

Once you have created an instance of the Line 6 Guitar Amp, press the Tab key to swing the device Rack around, and you'll see that the output of the audio track device has been routed to the input of the device.

The Effects of Record

Record includes 10 fantastic effects that are sure to get the job done for any band or singer/songwriter. In fact, you can expand those effects even more if you own other Propellerhead or Line 6 products, which I'll get into later.

Before beginning this section of the chapter, be sure to download the Record Ignite Demo song that I have prepared. As you take a listen, you'll hear that it doesn't really have a lot of pop or zing to it, which makes learning about the effect that much more fun. You'll use the Record effects to make this dull mix sound much better.

The RV7000 Reverb

The RV7000 is a true stereo professional reverb effect that sounds unreal. It has several different types of reverberation, along with an included EQ and Gate for shaping your reverb in ways that just can't be done by most hardware and software reverbs. You can use it to add depth to your vocal/guitar/drum parts and is best used as a send effect.

Try the following exercise. You're going to use the Main Mixer for this example, so press the F5 key to maximize it.

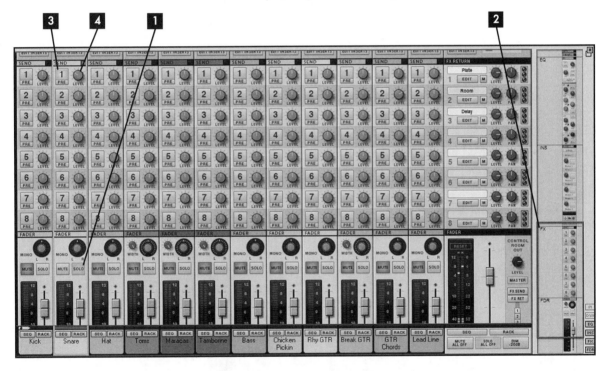

1 **Click** on the **Solo button** to solo the Snare track.

2 **Locate** the **FX sends** in the Channel Strip Navigator, which are just above the channel fader.

3 There are instances of the RV7000 loaded on FX sends 1 and 2. The first instance has a plate reverb loaded on it, while the second instance has a room reverb loaded on it. **Click** on the **first send button** to activate it.

4 **Adjust** the **Level knob** to set the amount of signal from the Snare track to the RV7000. It's pretty easy to go overboard with reverb, so just flavor it a little.

5 **Click** on the **Solo button** again to hear the rest of the mix.

The DDL-1 Delay

The DDL-1 is Record's built-in delay, which is used to repeat phrases, thicken up guitar or vocal parts, syncopate drums, and introduce a funky tempo feeling to your songs. Use this effect as a send effect, and the songs will practically write themselves.

Try the following exercise:

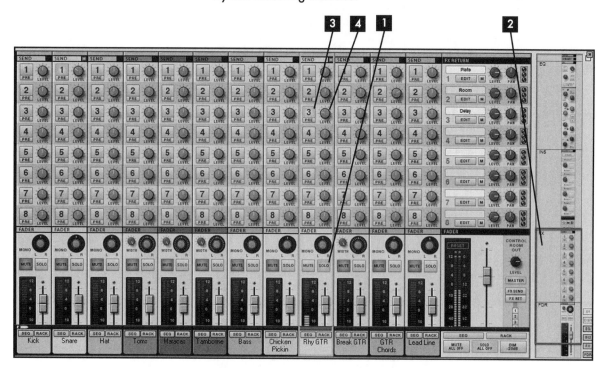

1 **Click** on the **Solo button** to solo the Rhy GTR track.

2 **Locate** the **FX sends** in the Channel Strip Navigator, which are just above the channel fader.

3 There's an instance of the DDL-1 loaded on FX send 3. **Click** on the **third send button** to activate it.

4 **Adjust** the **Level knob** to set the amount of signal from the Rhy GTR track to the DDL-1. Remember, a little delay goes a long way, so easy does it.

5 **Click** on the **Solo button** again to hear the rest of the mix.

As with the reverb, a delay can be easily overused in a song, so I would suggest setting it at a low value. Remember, you can always add more later.

The CF-101 Chorus/Flanger

A chorus/flanger effect is commonly used to add depth and ambience to a sound by introducing a short delay to the fed audio signal. That delayed signal is then mixed with the original dry signal, creating a much larger sound than before. The size and broadness of the delayed signal is determined by the set delay time, feedback, and LFO modulation. Listen to any old Phil Collins vocal part ("In the Air Tonight" is a good example), and you'll hear the chorus effect in full swing. If you want a great example of a flanger, try some old British metal, like Judas Priest. Those recordings were practically soaked in flangers.

For this exercise, let's use the CF-101 as an insert on another rhythm guitar track. Before beginning, turn on the Loop function; then set the left locator to bar 13 and the right locator to 17. Also, press the F5 key on your computer keyboard to show the device rack.

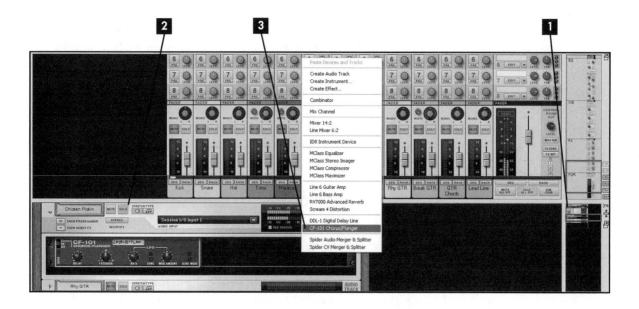

1 Use the Rack Navigator to locate the **Chicken Pickin audio track device**.

2 **Click** on the **Solo button** to solo the Chicken Pickin track.

3 Right-click on the Chicken Pickin audio track device and select **Create > CF-101 Chorus/Flanger**. This will place the instance of the CF-101 in the insert section of the Chicken Pickin audio track device.

4 **Click** on the **Solo button** again to hear the rest of the mix.

At this point, you can adjust the various parameters of the CF-101 to get the sound you like. Note that if you click on the Sync parameter, the Rate parameter can be changed in note values, rather than basic numeric values.

Before moving on, here's a handy tip. If you have the Main Mixer maximized and you want to jump to the Rack, you can do this quickly by navigating to the Rack button, which is found at the bottom of any mixer channel. Click on it to display the Rack and automatically jump to the rack device of the selected mixer channel.

The Scream 4 Digital Distortion

Although Record includes a great Line 6 amp modeling/distortion effect, the Scream 4 is a Propellerhead creation found in the Reason program. This effect will saturate, decimate, destroy, and mangle any audio that gets in its way and includes enough versatility that it can be used with just about any instrument. Be warned, Nine Inch Nails.

For this exercise, let's use the Scream 4 as an insert on the GTR Chords track. Before beginning, turn on the Loop function, then set the left locator to bar 21 and the right locator to 34.

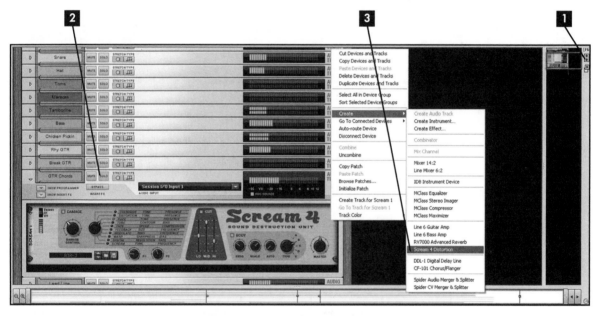

1 **Press F6** to maximize the Rack.

2 Use the Rack Navigator to locate the GTR Chords audio track device. Once you locate the device, **click** on its **Solo button**.

3 Right-click on the GTR Chords audio track device and **select Create > Scream 4 Distortion**.

The Scream 4 sounds pretty good with the default settings. However, I think you'll agree that it needs a few adjustments. When I put this song together, I was thinking of a guitar being heard through a telephone, which basically means that it's all mid-range with little-to-no low or high range. Let me show you how to achieve this with Scream 4.

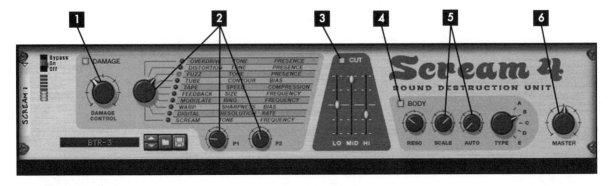

1 Set the **Damage Control knob** to 44.

2 Set the **Damage type** to Fuzz, and then set the **P1 knob** to approximately 24 and the **P2 knob** to approximately 52.

3 Activate the **Cut section** of Scream 4 and set Lo to 0, Mid to 56, and Hi to –23.

4 Activate the **Body section** of Scream 4 and set the Body Type to B.

5 Set the **Reso parameter** to 38 and the **Scale parameter** to 84.

6 Set the **Master** to approximately 65.

You can now click on the Solo buttons of all the soloed tracks to hear the entire mix.

The Line 6 Guitar and Bass Amps

These effects are a Record exclusive and were made possible by a collaboration of Propellerhead Software and Line 6. Those of you in the guitar world must know the name Line 6. They are the ground-breaking company that introduced the concept of *amp modeling*, which emulates the characteristics of popular hardware amps through software. With a Line 6 amp, you can make your guitar sound like its playing through any amp you've ever wanted but weren't able to find or afford (a common problem all of us guitar players face, I'm sure). All of that amp power is now available as part of Record for your guitar and bass tracks.

Try the following exercise:

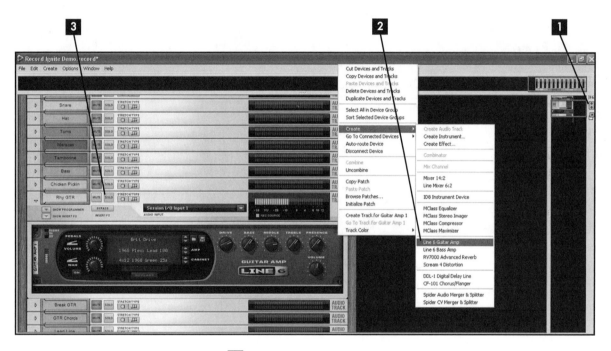

1 Use the Rack Navigator to **locate** the **Rhy GTR track device**. Once you locate the device, click on its Solo button.

2 Right-click on the Rhy GTR audio track device and **select Create > Line 6 Guitar Amp**.

3 **Click** on the **Solo button** again to hear the rest of the mix.

The default setting will work just fine for this example. Now let's do the same thing with the Bass track.

1 Use the Rack Navigator to **locate** the **Bass track device**. Once you locate the device, click on its Solo button.

2 Right-click on the Bass audio track device and select **Create > Line 6 Bass Amp**.

While the default setting is great for this track, it still needs a little more pump to it. Make the following adjustments to the Line 6 Bass Amp parameters.

1 Set the **Drive** to 17.

2 Set the **Bass** to 99.

3 Set the **Hi Mid** to 107

4 Set the **Treble** to 101.

5 **Click** on the **Solo button** again to hear the rest of the mix.

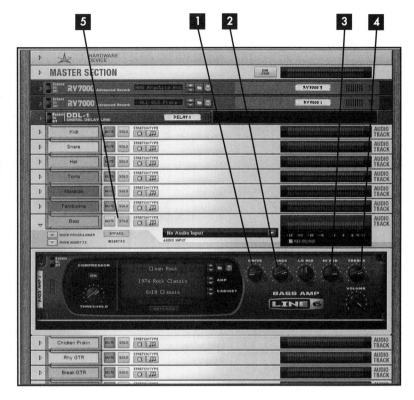

For this song, you'll also want to create an instance of the Line 6 Guitar Amp for the Lead Line track and select a preset that is different from the Rhy GTR track.

Try the following exercise:

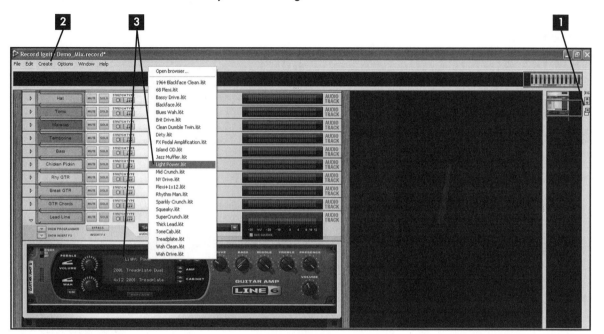

1 Use the Rack Navigator to **locate** the **Lead Line track device**. Once you locate the device, click on its Solo button, expand the device, and click on the Show Insert FX.

2 **Select Create > Line 6 Guitar Amp**. This will create an instance of the Line 6 Guitar Amp, and it will be automatically routed as an insert effect.

3 **Right-click** on the name of the currently loaded preset called **Brit Drive**. This will open a menu of the included presets of the Line 6 Guitar Amp. **Select** the **Light Power preset** to load it.

The MClass Suite

The MClass Suite is a compilation of four different effects that can be used individually with your Record tracks, or they can be used in combination with each other for the sole purpose of mixing and mastering. When you positively need to clean and polish every single track in your Record song, accept no substitutes. In these next few exercises, I'll show you how to use these effectively on individual tracks, and then I'll wrap things up by using them with the Combinator.

The MClass Equalizer

The MClass EQ functions well as an individual equalizer and as a mastering tool. It is a parametric equalizer that includes a graph to display your changes to the EQ curve as you make changes to the EQ's parameters. In this example, I'll use it on the Rhy GTR track.

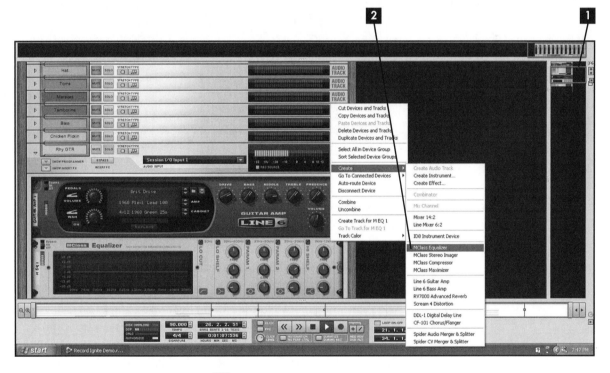

1 Use the Rack Navigator to **locate** the **Rhy GTR track device** and click on its Solo button.

2 Right-click on the Rhy GTR audio track device and **select Create > MClass Equalizer**. This will create an instance of the device and place it just below the Line 6 Guitar Amp.

Now, let's make a couple of adjustments to the EQ curve.

1 **Activate** the **39Hz–20kHz band** of the EQ.

2 **Set** the **Frequency** to 1.309 kHz.

3 **Set** the **Gain** to 7.4 dB.

4 **Set** the **Q** to 1.5.

5 **Click** on the **Solo button** to hear the rest of the mix.

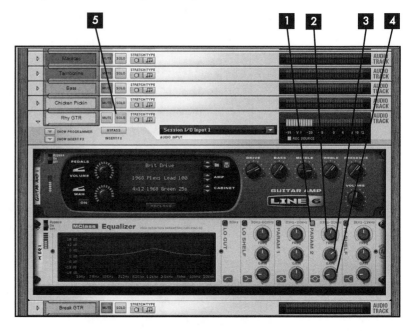

Here's a handy tip. Hold the Shift key down while making adjustments to any knobs on the Record interface. This will slow down the scroll rate of the knob.

The MClass Stereo Imager

The MClass Stereo Imager is used to help you achieve a deep and wide stereo image while preserving tight and defined bass in your mix. However, keep in mind that this effect will not create a stereo image of a mono track. It should be used with a stereo track and as an insert effect. Let's have a look at this with the Maracas track.

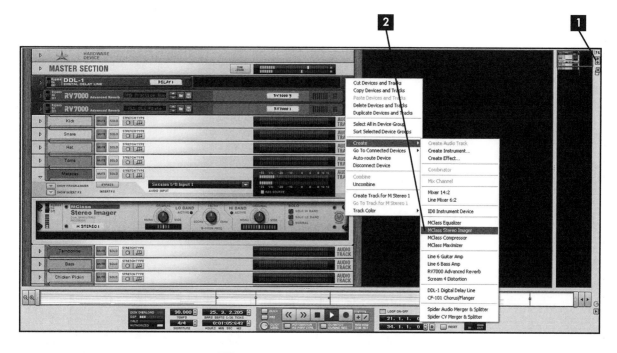

1 Use the Rack Navigator to **locate** the **Maracas track device** and click on its Solo button.

2 Right-click on the Maracas audio track device and **select Create > MClass Stereo Imager**.

Now, let's make a couple of adjustments to the stereo image.

1 Set the **Lo Band** to 45.

2 Set the **Hi Band** to 26.

If you want to really hear the results of this effect, use the Bypass switch, which is located all the way at the upper-left corner of the device. It's not a dramatic difference; rather, it has sweetened up the sound of the maracas. Click on the Solo button again to hear the rest of the mix.

The MClass Compressor

This is a single-band compressor, which can be used to prevent digital clipping in your mix, or it can be used to create really aggressive pumping effects on individual tracks. In this case, you're going to use the compressor on the Chicken Pickin track to create a plucky, crisp sound.

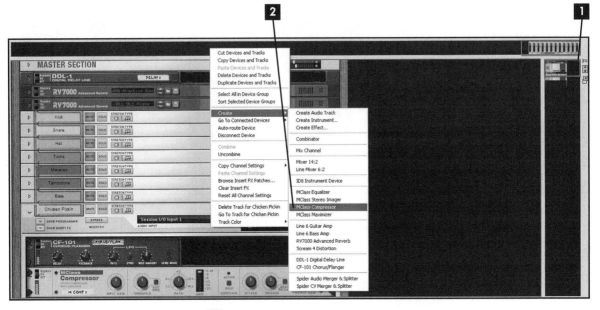

■1 Use the Rack Navigator to **locate** the **Chicken Pickin track device** and click on its Solo button.

■2 Right-click on the Chicken Pickin audio track device and **select Create > MClass Compressor**.

At this point, you'll notice that the compressor has been placed below the instance of the CF-101 that you created a few pages ago. This simply means that the audio track is going through the CF-101 first, and then the compressor. For this example, you need the compressor to come first, as you don't want to compress the chorus effect, just the dry track.

Let's have a little fun with this and make use of the back of the Rack. Select both the CF-101 and the MClass Compressor by using the Shift key on your computer keyboard and selecting Disconnect Devices from the Edit menu. Now press the Tab key to swing the Rack around and try the following exercise.

1 Click and drag a virtual cable from the Insert FX To Device L output of the audio track device to the Audio Input L of the MClass Compressor.

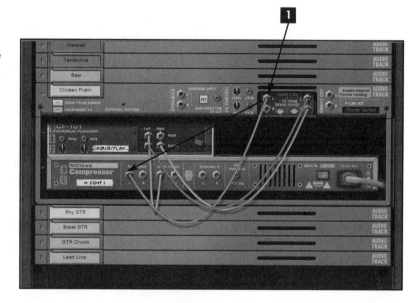

2 Click and drag a virtual cable from the Audio Output L from the MClass Compressor to the Left input of the CF-101.

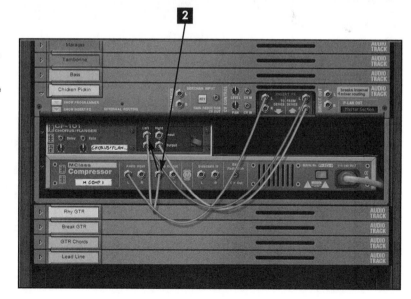

3 Click and drag a virtual cable from the Audio Output L of the CF-101 to the Insert FX From Device L input.

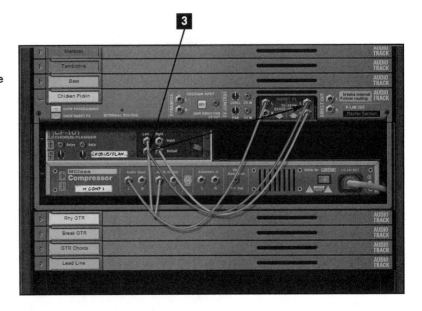

Press the Tab key to swing the Rack around again, and now let's make a couple of adjustments to the Compressor.

1 Set the Input Gain to 3.4 dB.

2 Set the Threshold to –30.6 dB.

3 Set the Ratio to 44.7:1.

4 Set the Attack to 24 ms.

5 Set the Output Gain to 4.1 dB.

6 Click on the Solo button to hear the rest of the mix.

The MClass Maximizer

The MClass Maximizer is a special type of limiter known as a *loud-ness maximizer*, which is used to significantly increase the perceived loudness of a mix without risking hard-clipping distortion. While it's best used on full mixes, it can work quite well with individual tracks. In this exercise, let's use it with the Snare track to give it a little more kick.

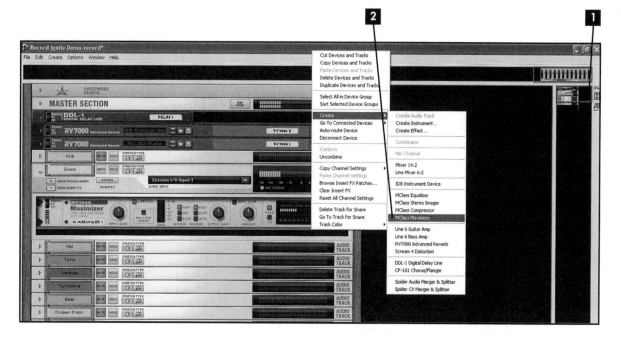

1 Use the Rack Navigator to **locate** the **Snare track device** and click on its Solo button.

2 Right-click on the Snare audio track device and **select Create > MClass Maximizer**.

At this point, be sure to save your song, as you are going to continue to use these effects in the next chapter.

Now make a couple of adjustments to the Maximizer.

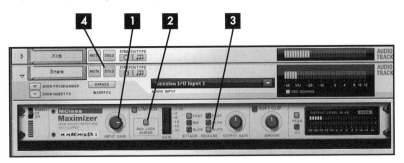

1 Set the **Input Gain** to 7.9 dB.

2 **Activate** the **4 ms Look Ahead**.

3 Set the **Release** to Auto.

4 **Click** on the **Solo button** to hear the rest of the mix.

The Combinator

The last effect I'll discuss is the Combinator, which isn't actually an effect. Rather, it's a device that allows you to compile virtually any combination of Record devices and save them as a single patch, known as a Combi. All of the compiled Record devices can then be controlled by a single Sequencer track. It's quite a clever, creative tool and is actually quite simple to use.

An Example of a Combinator Patch

There is actually an instance of the Combinator in the Record Demo Song within the Master Section device. Use the Rack Navigator to locate the Master Section device, expand it, and then click on the Show Programmer and Show Insert FX buttons. Also note that if you're using the Main Mixer, you can press the Edit Inserts button found in the Master Section, which will open the Rack and jump right to the Master Section device.

Now, let's load a Combi patch.

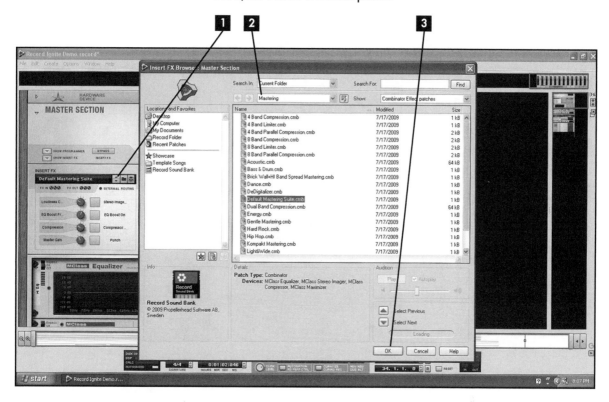

1 **Click** on the **Browse Insert FX Patch button** to launch the Insert FX Browser window.

2 **Select Mastering** from the presets pull-down menu, and select Default Mastering Suite.cmb. Note that when you select this patch, all of the effects within the Combi will show up in the Rack automatically.

3 **Click OK**, and the Combi patch will be loaded into the Record Rack.

Now that you have loaded a Combi Patch, take a moment to familiarize yourself with the layout of the Combinator.

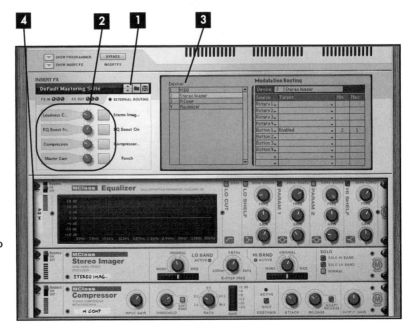

1 The Master Section patch browser is used to load and save different Combi patches. As you can see, this Combi is called the Default Mastering Suite.

2 The insert knobs and buttons are used to activate and alter specifically assigned parameters from within a Combi. In this example, knob 1 is used to alter the Loudness Curve, while button 1 is used to activate the Stereo Imager.

3 The Programmer is used to assign sources to specific parameters within a Combi. As you can see, the Stereo Imager is selected and button 1 is assigned to the Enable parameter of the Stereo Imager.

4 The Insert FX are the devices contained within a Combi. As you can see here, all of the MClass Mastering Suite effects are part of the Default Mastering Suite Combi.

As you are going to mix this song in the next chapter, let's take out the Mastering Suite for now so that you can begin mixing with as clean a slate as possible. Click on the Insert FX device of the Master Section and select Edit > Clear Insert FX. At this point, save your song so you're ready to move on. However, do not save your song again after going through the following exercise.

Building a Combinator Patch

In this final tutorial of the chapter, I'm going to show you how to create a very simple Combi patch and how to do a little bit of routing with the Combi Programmer.

Get yourself ready by activating the Loop function and setting your left and right locators to bars 25 and 29, respectively. Select and solo the Chicken Pickin audio track device, expand it, and try the following exercise:

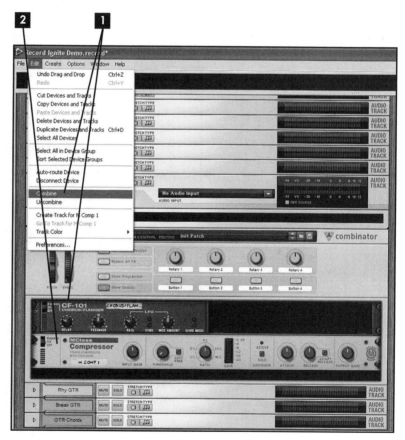

1 Click on the CF-101 to select it, and then **select Combine** from the **Edit menu**. This will create an instance of the Combinator and place the CF-101 within the device display of the Combinator.

2 **Click and drag** the MClass **Compressor** into the Combinator device display. This will place it just below the CF-101.

At this point, you have just created a very simple Combi patch, so let's keep building on it. Before you begin, right-click in the empty space next to the CF-101 and select Create > DDL-1 Delay.

Before proceeding to the next exercise, navigate to the DDL-1 and adjust the Dry/Wet knob to 24. This will give you a healthy mix of dry and wet signal.

At this point, you have created a simple Combi and loaded an additional effect. Now, let's look at how to set up the DDL-1 with the Combinator Programmer.

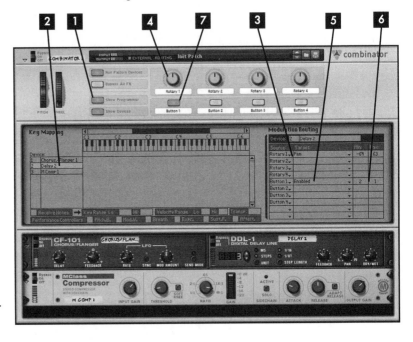

1. **Click** on the **Show Programmer button** to display the Combinator Programmer.

2. **Click** on the **DDL-1 Delay 2** in the Key Mapping list to select it.

3. To the right is the Modulation Routing list, which allows you to assign the buttons and knobs of the Combinator to specific device parameters (called targets) within a Combi. **Set Rotary 1** to **Pan** by selecting it from the Target pull-down menu.

4. If you **adjust** the **first knob on the Combinator**, you should now see it alter the Pan parameter of the DDL-1. This creates a fantastic stereophonic effect, as you'll be able to alter the panning of the delay reflections in real time. Note that you can double-click on the Rotary 1 label and rename it to whatever you wish.

5. **Set Button 1** to **Enabled** by selecting it from the Target pull-down menu.

6 **Assign** a **Min value** of 2 and a **Max value** of 1 to the Enabled target.

7 **Click** on **Button 1** of the Combinator, and you will see the DDL-1 Enable parameter switch between Bypass and On. Again, you can double-click on the Button 1 label and rename it to whatever you wish.

That's really all there is to starting your own Combi patch. There are far more in-depth tutorials on this device in the following books, both from Course Technology/Cengage Learning: *Propellerhead Record Power!* by Ernie Rideout (2010) and *Reason 4 Power!* by Yours Truly (2007).

8 } Mixing Your Record Song

Mixing requires you, as the artist, to switch hats from the musician to the engineer. This is the moment of truth, when you listen attentively to your recorded performances and decide how to best represent those performances in a stereo mix. That is the essence of mixing your song. For some artists, this in itself can represent weeks and possibly months before they get the sound they're after. Personally, I don't believe it should take that long to get a good mix of your song. While being a scrupulous mixer can produce some marvelous results, it can also risk making the overall sound of the song appear stale and uninspired. Remember, some of the greatest rock and pop songs were recorded and mixed within days. If they can do it, so can you!

Throughout this chapter, you're going to mix the Record Ignite Demo song by adding effects, using EQs, panning, and adjusting amplitudes. This will help give you the knowledge you'll need in order to mix your own songs.

Note that you'll continue to use the insert effects that you've been using up to this point, but the rest of the mix should be bone dry before beginning this chapter.

Applying EQ, Pan, and Levels

Before you start digging into setting up and using send effects like reverb and delay, you should first start the mix process by using the strict basics of equalization, panning, and levels. Doing this first will help you place the elements of your song in their proper places within the mix.

Mixing the Drums

When I start a mix, I like to work with the rhythm section first before attempting to carve out some space for the lead lines and vocals. Doing this will give you a good foundation for the rest of the song. Before beginning this series of exercises, do the following: Press the F5 key on your computer keyboard to maximize the view of the Main Mixer. Hide everything except the EQ and Fader sections by using the Hide/Show buttons at the bottom right of the Channel Strip Navigator. Simply click the buttons correlating to sections that you do not want to show. For example, if you don't want to show the dynamics, click the DYN button; it will grey out, and this section will no longer be visible in the Main Mixer. Set the left locator to bar 11, the right locator to bar 13, and turn on Loop mode so that you'll hear the drums consistently while you're mixing them.

Let's start with the Kick track. Solo this track, and try the following exercise.

1 **Activate** the **EQ section** for the Kick mixer channel.

2 **Set** the Low Mid Frequency **Gain** to approximately –7.30 dB.

3 **Set** the Low Mid **Frequency** to approximately 1.04 kHz.

4 **Set** the Low Mid Frequency **Q value** to 1.09.

5 **Set** the **Low Frequency Gain** to approximately 1.59 dB.

6 **Set** the **Fader slider** to approximately –4.61 dB.

As this point, you should have a nice boomy Kick drum track. Now try the following exercise on the Snare track. Solo this channel along with the Kick track.

1 **Activate** the **EQ section** for the Snare mixer channel.

2 **Set** the High Frequency **Gain** to approximately 7.62 dB.

3 **Set** the High **Frequency** to approximately 11.33 kHz.

4 **Set** the **High Mid Frequency Gain** to approximately –8.25 dB.

5 **Set** the **Fader slider** to approximately –6.36 dB.

Listening to the two tracks playing back should sound quite different from where you started a minute ago. To finish off this track, you'll want to pan the snare slightly to the left to help enhance the stereo mix. Set the Pan knob on the Snare track to approximately –34.

Let's now make some adjustments to the Hat track. Solo it along with the Kick and Snare tracks, and try the following exercise.

1 **Activate** the **EQ section** for the Hat track.

2 **Set** the High Frequency **Gain** to approximately 5.7 dB.

3 **Set** the High **Frequency** to approximately 9.94 kHz.

4 At this point, you'll also want to **adjust** the **Pan knob** and **Fader slider** to help the Hat track mix in with the other two tracks. Set the Pan to –60 and set the Fader to approximately –7.24 dB. That should give you a nice balanced mix between the three drum tracks.

Now you're going to mix the Toms track. Before beginning, set the left locator to bar 9 and the right locator to bar 11 so you'll be able to hear all four tracks. After you have done this, solo its track along with the Kick, Snare, and Hat tracks, and try the following exercise.

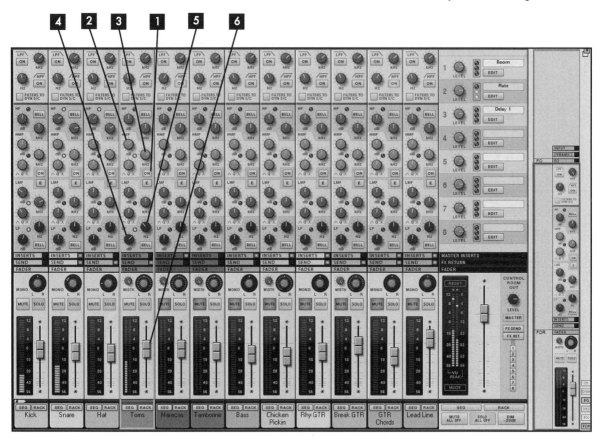

1 Activate the EQ section for the Toms track.

2 Set the High Mid Frequency Gain to approximately 5.08 dB.

3 Set the High Mid Frequency to approximately 3.80 kHz.

4 Set the Low Frequency Gain to approximately 5.40 dB.

5 Set the Low Frequency to approximately 110.7 Hz.

6 Set the Fader slider to approximately –3.86 dB.

At this point, you'll want to adjust the panning and level. In this case, since the Toms are on a stereo track, you'll want to adjust the Width parameter knob to specify how wide the stereo signal should be. By default, it's set to 127. This is the maximum setting. In this case, it might be a better idea to set it to a lower value in order to tighten up the stereo field, so I would adjust the width to approximately 68 to give it a generous stereo sound, but not so extreme.

Now you're going to push on and mix the Maracas and Tambourine. Before beginning, set the left locator to bar 23 and the right locator to bar 27.

The Maracas and Tambourine tracks were prepared audio loops that I had imported into Record when I was writing this track. As they already sound pretty decent, I don't think you'll need to do much to these two tracks. Solo their tracks along with the Kick, Snare, Hat, and Toms tracks, and make the following adjustments.

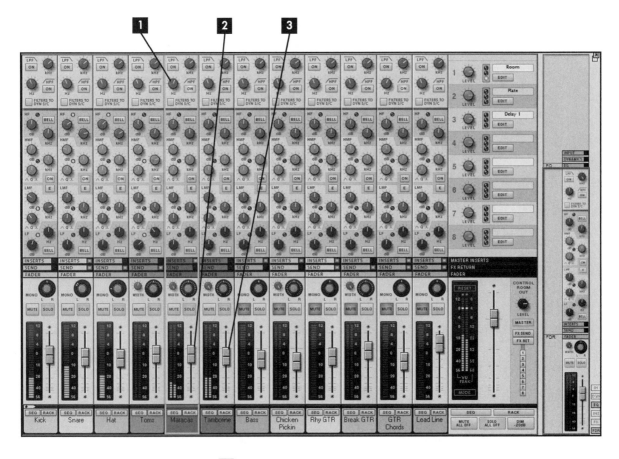

1. On the Maracas track, **activate** the **High Pass Filter** and set it to approximately 465 Hz. This is an EQ that allows high frequencies to pass while filtering out low frequencies.

2. Set the **Fader slider** of the Maracas track to approximately –4.02 dB.

3. Set the **Fader slider** of the Tambourine track to approximately –5.91 dB.

You have now made all of the proper adjustments to your drum tracks. You will revisit these tracks later in the chapter when you start applying send effects to the mix.

Mixing the Bass

The bass is a tricky instrument to mix, as you need to achieve two goals:

- ✳ Make it sound punchy and focused.
- ✳ Have it complement the rhythm section, not overwhelm it.

More often than not, I'll hear mixes where the bass completely takes over the low end of the song. And while it might seem like a great thing with certain styles of music, what it typically ends up doing is making the mix sound squishy and helps lose the focus of the song.

To make sure this doesn't happen is first to make sure the bass is recorded properly. It doesn't need to be over-compressed or equalized when you record it. Just get a good, solid bass sound and let the Main Mixer do the rest.

Solo the Bass track by itself and make the following adjustments.

1 Activate the **EQ section** for the Bass track.

2 Set the High Frequency **Gain** to approximately 7.62 dB.

3 Set the **Low Mid Frequency Gain** to approximately 3.81 dB.

4 Set the **Low Frequency Gain** to approximately 1.27 dB.

5 Set the **Fader slider** to approximately –8.09 dB.

At this point, you have added a little more meat to the overall bass sound. All that's left to be done is set the Fader, as you won't need to pan the bass. However, if you solo the rest of the drums and listen to how great the bass sounds along with them, I think you'll agree that the bass sounds fine if left at –8.09 dB on the Main Mixer. You can change this later, but you will risk overwhelming the mix.

Mixing the Rhythm and Lead Guitars

In this next section, you're going to mix the three rhythm guitar tracks. Each of these guitar tracks are unique to the overall vibe of the song. For example, the main rhythm guitar track, called Rhy GTR, is meant to be the foundation of the song. The main chords of the song are found on this track, so it is probably the most important of this group of tracks in the mix. The GTR Chords track and Chicken Pickin tracks are meant to introduce different elements into the song. The Chicken Pickin track is meant to be a plucky, brittle, country-esque rhythm part that complements the bass track. The GTR Chords track is meant to be a low-fidelity rhythm track that adds chord variations on top of the main chords of the song. Additionally, this track is meant to move from left to right and back again in the stereo mix of the song, which can be accomplished by using automation, which you will do later in this chapter.

For now though, let's get the mix right on these tracks, starting with the Chicken Pickin track. Set the left locator to 15 and the right locator to 34 and make sure the Loop function is still active. Solo the Chicken Pickin track, along with the bass and drums, and make the following adjustments.

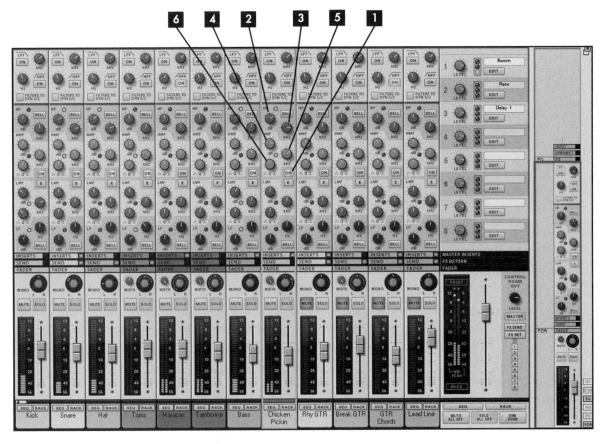

1. **Activate** the **EQ section** for the Chicken Pickin track.

2. **Set** the High Frequency **Gain** to approximately 7 dB.

3. **Set** the High **Frequency** to approximately 12.79 kHz.

4. **Set** the **High Mid Frequency Gain** to approximately 9.52 dB.

5. **Set** the **High Mid Frequency** to approximately 3.80 kHz.

6. **Set** the High Mid Frequency **Q value** to approximately 1.21.

At this point, the Chicken Pickin track should sound plucky and brittle. You can now complete the mix on this track by adjusting the Pan to 41 and the Fader to approximately –10.16 dB. This will place the track over to the right in the stereo field, and it will complement the level of the Bass track nicely.

Next up is the main rhythm guitar track, called Rhy GTR. This track already sounds pretty good as is and mixes well with the other tracks. It would be a good idea to give this track just a little more sizzle on the high end and make a couple of panning and level adjustments. Solo its track, and try the following exercise.

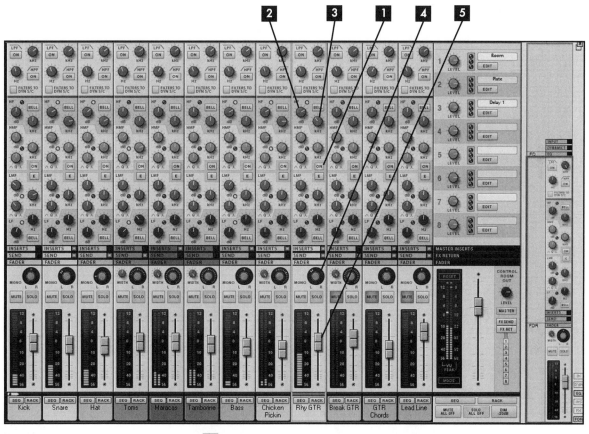

1 **Activate** the **EQ section** for the Rhy GTR track.

2 **Set** the High Frequency **Gain** to approximately 7.94 dB.

3 **Set** the High **Frequency** to approximately 4.11 kHz.

4 **Set** the **Pan knob** to approximately –25.

5 **Set** the **Fader slider** to approximately –3.94 dB.

The next track you're going to mix is the GTR Chords track. As mentioned before, the purpose of this track is to act as a low-fidelity rhythm guitar track that plays chord variations on top of the Rhy GTR track. The goal is then to make this track identifiable in the mix but not be the dominant track. Solo its track and make the following adjustments.

1 Activate the **High Pass Filter**.

2 Set the High Pass Filter **Frequency** to approximately 432.1 Hz.

At this point, you will have filtered out all of the low and mid frequencies, and that's perfect for using this song. You can also set the fader on this track to -9.80 dB, which will pull it back a little in the mix. Later on in this chapter, you'll add some panning automation to this track and a nice reverb to give it a completely new texture.

The last adjustment you'll make to the rhythm guitar tracks is to solo the Break GTR and set its Fader to -1.50 dB. This track is only used one time in the song, and as such, it doesn't need any EQ adjustments, just volume. At this point, you can click on the Solo All Off button, which is found at the bottom of the Master fader. This will un-solo all of the tracks so that you can hear your mix.

The final track you'll mix is the Lead Line track. Like a vocal track, this is the most important track of the mix—it introduces a melody into the song, so it really needs to stand out in front of the mix. This can be accomplished by using a combination of EQ, pan, and volume.

Make the following adjustments to the EQ:

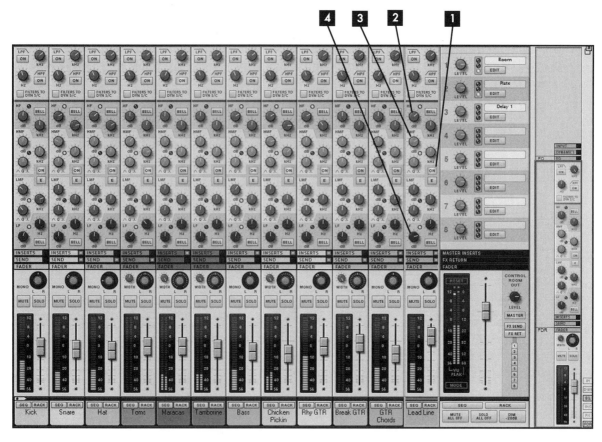

1 **Activate** the **EQ section** for the Lead Line track.

2 **Set** the High Frequency **Gain** to approximately 6.67 dB.

3 **Set** the **High Mid Frequency Gain** to approximately 7.62 dB.

4 **Set** the **Low Frequency Gain** to approximately 9.21 dB.

 The final adjustments you'll make to this track are to the Pan and Volume. Set the Pan to approximately 12 and the Fader slider to approximately 2.70 dB. This will skew the track to the right a little bit and make it stand out from of the rest of the mix.

Adding Send Effects to the Mix

If you listen to the song thus far, you have created a really great-sounding mix that's pretty dry and barebones. Believe me; you've already achieved a lot more than most people would their first time out with mixing a song. Now you're going to the next step, setting up some effects and adding them to your mix. Before you begin, hide the EQ section of the Main Mixer and show the FX section.

As you'll recall from the previous chapter, you already created two instances of the RV7000 Reverb and the DDL-1 delay. The final send effect you'll want to use for this chapter is a Tape delay.

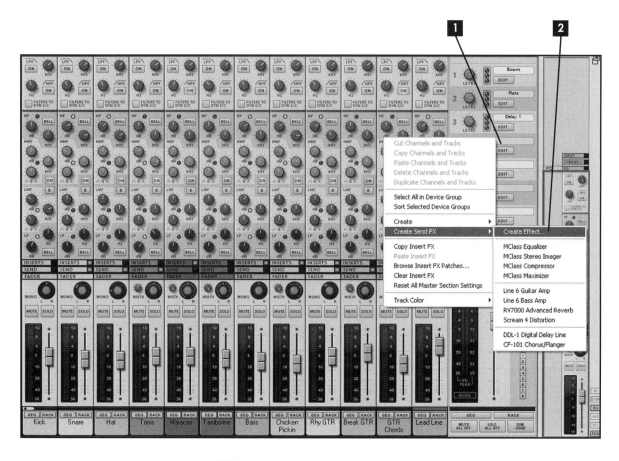

1 **Navigate** your **mouse** to the FX Return of the Main Mixer.

2 **Right-click** on the **fourth FX return**, and select Create Send FX > Create Effect. This will open the Patch Browser.

3 **Double-click** on **Effect Patches**, and this will give you access to all of the different categories of effect patches that have been prepared for you in Record. All of these different effects have been created using the different devices of Record along with the Combinator to give you combinations that would otherwise be quite difficult to accomplish.

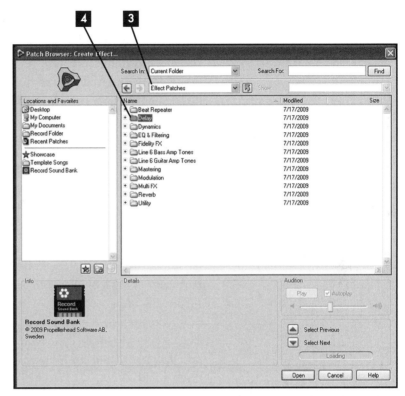

4 **Double-click** on the **Delay folder**, and then double-click on the Stereo Delay folder. You will see nine different stereo delay presets at your disposal. Double-click on the Stereo Tape Delay, and this will load the preset into FX Return 4. You can double-click on FX Return 4 and rename it **Stereo Delay** to help keep your effects organized.

That's really all you need to get a good mix happening. Remember that while you have all of the power of Record at your fingertips, you don't want to overdo it. The temptation is always there, but you don't want your song sounding like it was mixed in a washing machine.

Applying Send Effects to the Drums

When using send effects with drums, it can be a slippery slope. There are certain drums that you're going to want to effect and others that you should avoid. For example, a kick drum really doesn't need to have either reverb or delay, except maybe for creative purposes. The snare drum however, is an instrument that just begs for reverb and a touch of delay if you want.

Just keep in mind that this is all subjective, as mixing is a feeling as well as a technical part of the recording process. Sure, there are rules of recording that should be followed, but if it sounds right, that's okay, too.

Since you applied some reverb to the Snare track in the last chapter, let's start with applying send effects to the Hat and Toms tracks. Also make sure to click on the FX button at the bottom right so you can see the FX Send area of the Main Mixer. Additionally, click on the EQ button to hide the EQ section of the Main Mixer, which will help free up some room on the Record interface. Set the left locator to 17 and the right locator to 20, and turn on the Loop function. Solo the drum tracks, press Play, and make the following adjustments.

1 **Activate** the **FX Send 1 button** on the Hat track.

2 **Activate** the **FX Send 2 button** on the Toms track.

3 **Set** the **FX Send 1 Level knob** to approximately –13.31 dB. This will assign some of the Hat track to the RV7000.

4 **Set** the **FX Send 2 Level knob** to approximately 0.77 dB. This will assign some of the Toms track to the RV7000.

That should do it for the drum tracks. If you want to come back and add some more effects to your drum mix, you should probably wait until after you finish mixing the rest of the song.

Applying Send Effects to the Guitars

Now let's add some effects to the guitar parts of the song. As with the drums, there are a couple of tracks that do not need any effects applied to them, namely the Bass and Chicken Pickin tracks. If you solo these tracks and listen to them closely, you'll notice that the Bass track already has a solid sound; the Chicken Pickin track already has a chorus and a delay applied to it, so adding any more effects to this track might make it sound a little too unfocused for the mix.

At this point, you can click on the Solo All Off button, which is found at the bottom of the Master Section fader. This will un-solo all of the tracks so you can hear your mix. You can also turn off the Loop function for now if you like. Follow along with the next steps to make adjustments to the guitar tracks.

1 Activate the **FX Send 1 button** on the Rhy GTR track.

2 Set the **FX Send 1 Level knob** to approximately –24.54 dB. This will assign some of the Rhy GTR track to the RV7000.

3 Activate the **FX Send 1 button** on the Break GTR track.

4 Set the **FX Send 1 Level knob** to approximately –16.54 dB. This will assign some of the Break GTR track to the RV7000.

5 Activate the **FX Send 1 and FX Send 4 buttons** on the GTR Chords track.

6 Set the **FX Send 1 knob** to approximately –19.67 and the **FX Send 4 knob** to –21.99. This will assign some of the GTR Chords track to the RV7000 and Stereo Delay, respectively.

7 Activate the **FX Send 1 and FX Send 3 buttons** on the Lead Line track.

8 Set the **FX Send 1 Level knob** to approximately –13.75 and the **FX Send 3 Level knob** to –28.89. This will assign some of the Lead Line track to the RV7000 and Delay 1, respectively.

Listening back to the song at this point, you should have a great-sounding solid mix. Now that you've gone through the exercises in this chapter, you can go back and make further adjustments if you want.

Adding Automation to the Mix

In this part of the chapter, you're going to add some automation to the song by using the Record Sequencer. You're only going to do a couple of simple automation moves, which will give you a great foundation to build on.

Automating the Pan

In this exercise, you're going to create an automation performance for the pan of the GTR Chords track. This will cause the GTR Chords track to pan from left to right in the stereo mix. Press the F7 key on your computer keyboard to maximize the Record Sequencer and then select the GTR Chords track.

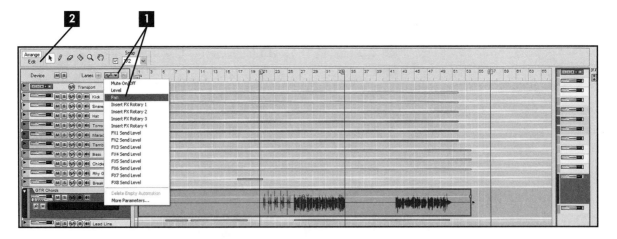

1 First, create an automation lane for the track. **Click** on the **Track Parameter Automation button** and select Pan. This will create a Pan automation lane on the GTR Chords track.

2 Now **click** on the **Edit button** to activate Edit mode.

Now you're ready to draw in some automation data. Try the following exercise:

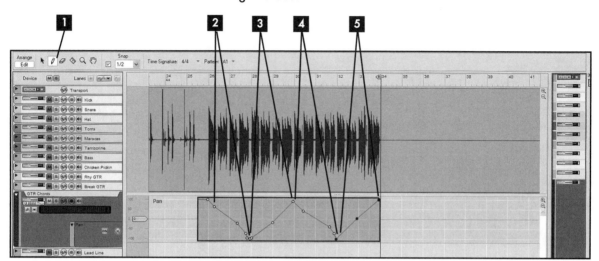

1 Select the **Pencil tool**.

2 Starting at bar 26 on the Pan lane, **click and drag down and diagonally to the right** until you reach bar 28. Release the mouse.

3 Starting at bar 28, **click and drag upward and diagonally to the right** until you reach bar 30. Release the mouse.

4 Starting at bar 30 on the Pan lane, **click and drag down and diagonally to the right** until you reach bar 32. Release the mouse.

5 Starting at bar 32 on the Pan lane, **click and drag up and diagonally to the right** until you reach bar 34. Release the mouse.

Now press F5 to maximize the Main Mixer and listen to the song. As the position indicator reaches bar 26, you'll see the Pan knob move back and forth. You'll also see a neon green frame around the knob, which tells you that there is automation data written to the track.

In this next exercise, you're going to add an additional automation lane to the GTR Chords track and draw in a quick automation curve. Press F7 to maximize the Sequencer, then click again on the Track Parameter Automation button and select FX1 Send Level. This will create a new automation lane just below the Pan lane. Now try the following exercise.

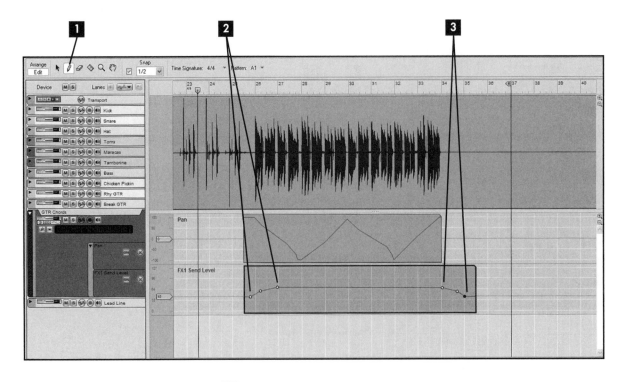

1 Select the **Pencil tool**.

2 Click between bars 25 and 26 **and drag an automation curve** that ends at about a value of 70 at bar 27.

3 Navigate to bar 34, at which point you can **click and drag an automation curve** that ends at about a value of 47 at bar 35. Then release the mouse.

Mastering Your Mix

The last topic of this chapter covers a quick way to master your mix by making use of the Master Inserts of the Main Mixer. These inserts, which are made up of Combi patches, govern the entire mix of your song, and they should be thought of and used as a finishing touch.

Press the F5 key on your computer keyboard and hide everything on the mixer except for the Inserts (INS) and the FX.

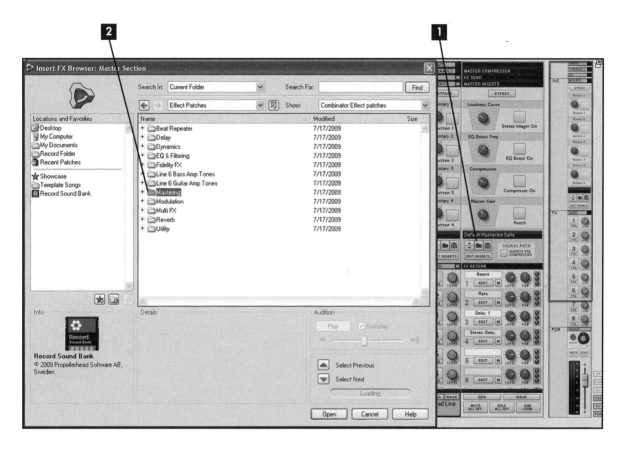

1 **Click** on the **Browse Insert FX Patch button**, and this will launch the Insert FX Browser window.

2 Double-click on Effect Patches, then **click** on the **Mastering folder**. Locate the Default Mastering Suite preset, and click OK to load it into the Master Inserts area. This Combi patch includes just about all of the MClass mastering effects. Once loaded in, you can use the knobs of the Master Inserts section to flavor and master your mix.

You should notice a pretty extreme difference in your mix at this point. If you click on the Edit Inserts button, this will display the Default Mastering Suite, which is loaded into the Master Section device in the Rack. You can click on the Bypass button of the Master Section device to turn the Default Mastering Suite on and off so you can hear the before and after effects. If you're not happy with the sound of the Default Mastering Suite, you can always select another mastering Combi patch by repeating the previous exercise. There are a few Combi patches that will sound pretty decent with this song, including the 4 Band Compression Combi or the Light and Wide Combi. As you finish this up, you're ready to move on to the next chapter, which talks about exporting your song.

9 ♬ Exporting Your Song

Now comes the moment you've been waiting for. You've worked your master-piece through and through, and you're ready to release your newly recorded hot single and start hitting the road to promote it. Dancing girls, wine, and backstage passes galore! Oh, by the way, the 80s called and they want their stereotypical lifestyle back.

Okay, maybe I'm overselling it a tad, but this is still an important moment for you as a user of Record. This is the moment you are going to export your song to one or several different solutions. This chapter is going to help you understand what your choices are and how to accomplish your goal quickly.

The term *exporting audio* is also commonly known as an *audio mixdown*, which is the process of combining all of the audio tracks, MIDI tracks, and real-time effects in your Record song into a single stereo digital audio file. This file can then be used to make an audio CD that can be played in any CD player. In addition to this, Record offers another solution for those of you who have friends that you jam and record with, but they don't have the same program on their computer. There's a unique way to collaborate with them that I will get into shortly.

Exporting Your Song as an Audio File

The first type of export I'll show you is the standard export, in which your entire song is mixed down to a single stereo audio file. This is most likely the export option you're going to use 99% of the time in Record.

Before starting the exercises of this chapter, be sure to load up the Record Demo Song. To get started, go to File > Export Song As Audio File. The Export Song As Audio File dialog box will appear.

1 Select the location where you want to save your exported file. For the sake of simplicity, I would suggest saving your song to the Desktop. Note that this screen looks slightly different on a Mac, but it's still pretty much the same procedure.

2 Give your song a name in the File Name field.

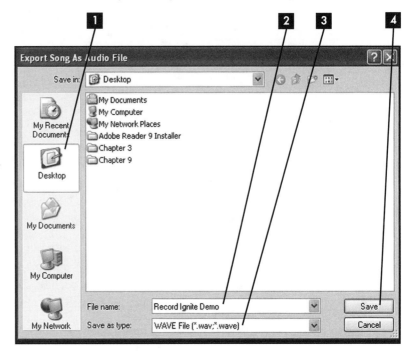

3 Choose a file format for your song. Record can export either AIFF or WAV files. The golden rule has previously been WAV files for Windows and AIFF for Macs. However, with today's computers, this is generally not much of a concern because most programs can support and open both WAV and AIFF files. The choice is really up to you.

4 Click Save.

Once you click Save, the Export Audio Settings dialog box appears, asking you to specify the sample rate and bit depth. Before you fill in the blanks, let me explain these very briefly.

The term *sample rate* by its simplest definition is the rate at which an audio signal is captured and converted to digital information. The rate that these bits are captured is described as a frequency measured in kilohertz (kHz). The sample rate of a prerecorded audio CD is 44.1 kHz; while this is the norm, there are several other sample rates available in Record, from 11 kHz to 192 kHz. However, unless you know for a fact that you need to use these other sample rates, you're most likely going to use 44.1 kHz all of the time.

There are some fantastic benefits to using Record with a higher sampling rate, as it will allow you to capture more frequencies while you record. This is especially useful when recording instruments that have a wide frequency range, such as a piano or crash cymbals. Just keep in mind that the higher the sampling rate, the more taxing it will be on your computer. Additionally, make sure that you have plenty of extra hard drive space, as recording at a higher sampling rate will eat up drive space for breakfast.

The last thing to keep in mind about using a higher sampling rate with Record is that you will eventually need to convert your song to a file that has a sampling rate of 44.1 kHz. This can be done in Record when you export your song, and there are a number of mastering programs available at your local music store such as WaveLab, Sound Forge, and Peak.

The term *bit depth* relates to the number of data bits that are needed in order to accurately capture analog signals at different amplitudes. These data bits are represented in a simple binary language of zeros and ones. While a prerecorded audio CD has a standard bit depth of 16 bits, the professional recording studio typically records audio at a much higher bit depth, usually 24 bits.

However, at the end of the day, you'll be exporting your songs to a bit depth of 16 by using a function called *dithering*. Dithering helps to smoothly convert your 24-bit audio to 16-bit audio by removing bits without creating an audible effect. Without dithering, the excess bits are simply truncated, or cut off, which can result in a harsher sound or a loss of perceived ambience. Dithering will smooth out these harsh mathematics by adding a barely perceptible amount of noise (random bits) at the very bottom of the noise floor in the upper frequencies of the audible range.

Try the following exercise:

1 In the Export Audio Settings dialog box, **set the Sample Rate value** to 44,100 Hz (also known as 44.1 kHz).

2 **Set** your **Bit Depth value** to 16 bits.

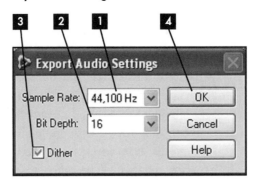

3 Make sure to **select Dither** so that your exported song will sound its best.

4 **Click** on the **OK button.**

At this point, Record will start exporting your song to the specified destination. You will see a window indicating that Record is exporting the song one bar at a time. Once this is done, you should be able to find your exported song on your computer Desktop.

Exporting Your Loop as an Audio File

Record can also export just portions of your songs as smaller audio files, more commonly called *loops*. Record does this by exporting whatever content is between the left and right locators. This is extremely useful for creating high-quality loops for creative usage in either Record or other DAW applications, like Pro Tools, Logic, Cubase, and SONAR. You could also import your newly created audio loops into the virtual sampler of Propellerhead's other program, Reason. This offers up some interesting remix possibilities.

Before you export your loop as an audio file, you need to make sure that you have set up your loop points in the Record Sequencer. Assuming you're using the Record Demo Song, make the following adjustments:

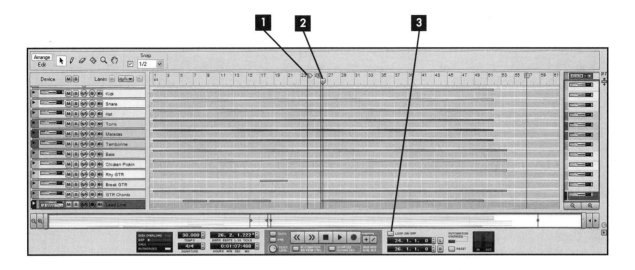

1 Using your mouse, you can either **click and drag** the **left locator** to bar 24 or double-click in the left locator dialog and type in bar 24.

2 Using the same method as step 1, **set** the **right locator** to bar 26.

3 At this point, you can **turn on** the **Loop function** and listen to how it sounds. If you're not happy with it or want to loop another part of the song, set up your left and right locators as needed.

At this point, you can now select Export Loop as Audio File from the File menu.

1 In the Export Loop as Audio File dialog box, **select** the **location** where you want to save your exported file. As was the case with the previous section, I would suggest saving your loop to the Desktop.

2 **Give** your **loop file** a name in the File Name field.

3 **Choose** a **file format** for your song. Record can export either AIFF or WAV files.

4 **Click Save.**

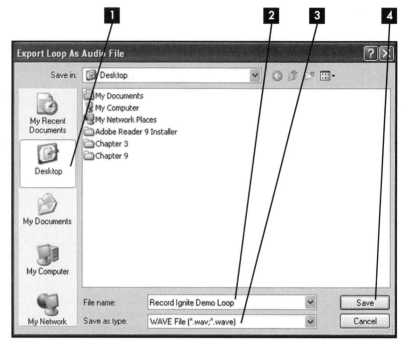

The next thing you'll need to do is set the loop's bit depth and sample rate.

1 Set your **Sample Rate value** to 44,100 Hz (also known as 44.1 kHz).

2 Set your **Bit Depth value** to 16 bits.

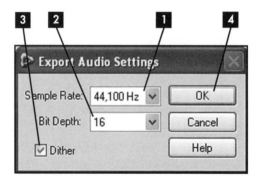

3 Make sure to **select Dither** so that your exported song will sound its best.

4 **Click** on the **OK button.**

Record Doesn't Create MP3s

MP3 is a digital audio file format used primarily to exchange music between friends, family, and, most important, your loyal listeners. It is a popular format because it compresses a high-quality stereo AIFF or WAV file to a much smaller size that can be transferred easily via the Web.

Record does not create MP3 files, although there are many MP3 encoding programs available at little or no cost. For example, Apple's iTunes encodes MP3 files like a champ and is available for both Mac and PC!

Bouncing Mixer Channels

A fairly unique feature to Record is the ability to export, or "bounce," all of the mixer tracks as separate audio files. These files can then be brought into other programs for further editing. This function makes Record a perfect application for collaboration between friends and band mates.

Select File > Bounce Mixer Channels and try the following exercise.

1 From the Mixer Channels list, **select** the **tracks** you want to bounce. You can select individual mixer tracks, the Master Section, and the FX channels. To speed things up, you can click on the Check All or Uncheck All button.

2 The Range to Bounce options are used to specify what you would like to bounce. You can **select Song**, which will bounce all channels from start to finish in the song, or you can **select Loop**, which will just bounce channels between the left and right locators. If you plan on providing your bounced audio files to another user for collaboration, make sure that Song is selected, as it will create audio files that are exactly the same length, which will allow the other user to import them into their audio application and the files will line up perfectly.

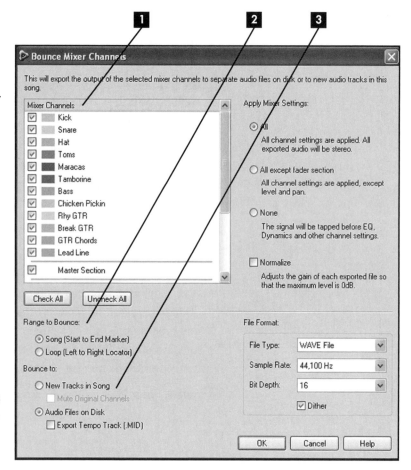

3 The Bounce To function is used to specify how you would like to handle the bounced audio tracks. You can **select New Tracks in Song**, which means that Record will bounce the audio and place that audio on new tracks within the original song. Note that you can mute the original track by selecting Mute Original Channels. You can also **select Audio Files on Disk**, which means that Record will create a new folder and place the bounced audio files within that folder. Additionally, Record can also export the tempo track as a MIDI file. This is an important feature, as you can import these bounced audio files into a new song in a different program, which means you will want the tempo to adjust accordingly. You might also want to hand over your project to a producer or engineer, who will want the MIDI file.

4 The **Apply Mixer Settings options** specify what you would like Record to bounce. You can choose between All, All Except Fader Section (the level and pan are ignored), or None (none of the Record mixer settings will be applied to the audio files). This can be helpful when collaborating with another user who might have different ideas of how to mix your song or have different audio effects they would like to apply to your song.

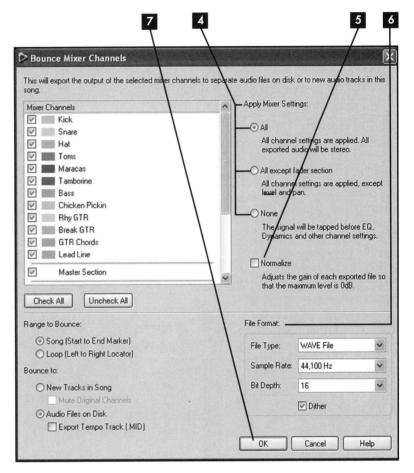

5 The **Normalize option** is used to export all of the bounced audio as normalized audio. *Normalization* simply means that Record will examine the audio file, find the loudest point, and then adjust the remaining audio around it to ensure that the bounced audio is louder than the original. This is a good feature to use, but be warned: This will also increase the volume of any track noise that may be included in the original recordings.

6 The **File Format options** (File Type, Sample Rate, Bit Depth, and Dither) are exactly like the export options you saw earlier in this chapter. If you are collaborating with someone else, make sure that you know the correct file type, sample rate, and bit depth to use.

7 Once you've made your selections, **click OK**, and Record will begin to bounce the mixer channels accordingly. This will probably take a few minutes, so be patient.

Exporting your song in Record is a snap, and as you have seen throughout this chapter, the Export tools can really help to promote collaboration between musicians, producers, and engineers. The resulting mix of your song may be completely different from what your producer or bandmate might have come up with, and that's a great option to have, as there are virtually limitless possibilities when mixing and remixing songs.

Appendix } An Overview of Reason

If you are new to recording music on your computer, you may not know about Record's big brother, Reason. This appendix will present a brief overview of Reason's main features and give you some idea of how the two programs work together. To learn more about Reason, check out *Reason 4 Ignite!* or *Reason 4 Power!*, both published by Cengage Learning.

Reason is music composition software that was first released by Propellerhead in 2000. It supplies the best of both software synthesis and sequencing for creative music production aimed at the electronic music scene. Within Reason lies the capability to produce, sequence, and professionally mix and master electronic music that consists of elements from glossy synth leads to bumpin' bass lines to hot and heavy drum loops.

Much of Record's layouts and graphical interface features were first conceived in Reason several years ago. However, the one big difference is that Record can record audio, while Reason does not. Conversely, Reason excels at soft synth music composition, while Record is very basic. When it comes down to it, you can combine both of these programs to get one powerful music-making machine. Best part is, it's not complicated. You simply install Reason, and when you launch Record, all of the Reason instruments and effects are integrated into the Record interface. No additional software, no workarounds—just simplicity.

Download the Reason Demo

You can download and install the demo version of Reason 4 by visiting the Propellerhead Software website (www.propellerheads.se). Once you install the Reason 4 demo, you'll be able to use it with Record. However, you can only use Record in the Demo mode when using it with the Reason demo. And hey, should you feel the need to get yourself a copy of Reason after going through this appendix (I dare you to not love it), you'll be happy to know that Propellerhead offers a discount to Record users. Just tell them Michael sent you (well, maybe not...).

Opening Reason Songs within Record

The first exercise you're going to do in this appendix is open a Reason song within Record. If you're familiar with Reason 4, you probably have some experience using Reason with other DAW programs (Pro Tools, Cubase, Logic, and so on) with ReWire. While this was groundbreaking technology for its time, ReWire is a bit cumbersome and in some cases requires a few extra steps. Thankfully, I think you'll find that using Reason and Record together is remarkably easier, as it is as simple as opening a Reason song right from within Record.

Launch Record and try the following exercise:

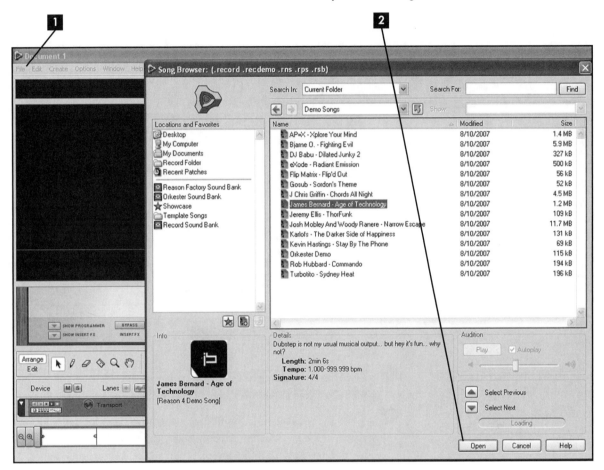

1 Select **File > Open** to open the Song Browser.

2 Locate a Reason song and **click** the **Open button**.

Now that you've opened your Reason song within Record, let's see
how Record has integrated the tracks and devices of Reason into
the Record interface.

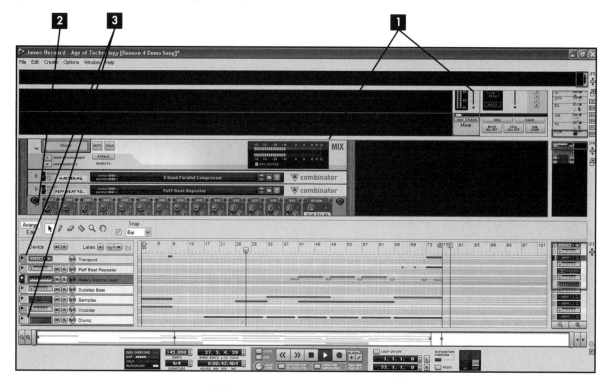

1 A single stereo channel has been created in the Record Main Mixer. This channel is linked to the Mix Channel device in the Record Device Rack.

2 All of the devices used in the Reason song have been loaded into Record. The outputs of the Reason mixer, called reMix, have been routed to the Mix Channel device. Press the Tab key on your computer keyboard to swing the Rack around to see how reMix has been routed to the Mix Channel device.

3 All of the Sequencer tracks from the Reason song have been loaded into Record.

At this point, you can create a new audio track and record some guitar, bass, drums, or vocals over your Reason song without a hitch.

The Instruments of Reason

Another great benefit to having both Reason and Record on the same computer is the ability to use all of the instruments and effects from Reason in your Record productions. After working with the effects and instruments provided in Record, having these new sounds and textures at your fingertips will expand your creative palette.

If you want to use Reason's synths and effects, just select any of them from the Create menu in Record. It's that simple.

The Subtractor Analog Synth

The Subtractor is a polyphonic synthesizer modeled after a classic hardware analog synth. It includes two oscillators and a noise generator for producing tones, in addition to dual filters, Low-Frequency Oscillators (or LFOs), and envelopes for shaping and editing the tones. The Subtractor also features a wide range of polyphony, which limits and expands the number of possible simultaneous notes generated. And just in case you're not a synth tweaker by nature, the Subtractor comes with many presets that will satisfy your creativity for a long time to come.

The Thor Polysonic Synth

The Thor Polysonic synth is by far the most complex soft synth found in Reason. This bad boy is a semi-modular synth that uses subtractive, wavetable, phase modulation, frequency modulation, multi-oscillation, and noise to create sounds. Additionally, Thor also provides a step sequencer, real-time effects and filters, and an impressive modulation bus, all of which can be routed in a variety of ways. You think it, and Thor can create it.

The Malstrom Graintable Synth

The Malstrom is one of Reason's more eclectic synths, as it houses a unique form of synthesis known as *graintable*, which is essentially a combination of granular and wavetable synthesis. This enables Malstrom to be your "go-to" synth for creating exceptional lead lines, dreamy pads, and ear-shattering bass lines.

The NN-19 and NN-XT Digital Samplers

The NN-19 and NN-XT are Reason's samplers. Both of these devices excel at emulating real sounds, such as strings, horns, and voices. This is all done by making use of clips of digital audio known as *samples*.

The Dr:rex Loop Player

Dr:rex is a sample playback device based on the ReCycle! technology created by Propellerhead Software. Dr:rex can import specially prepared digital audio loops, called REX files, and play them back at just about any tempo. Additionally, any REX loops loaded into Dr:rex will change with the tempo of the song.

The Redrum Drum Computer

Redrum is Reason's virtual drum machine. When you create an instance of it, you'll see that it's split into two sections. The top part of the interface is where you work with the individual percussion sounds. Each sound is assigned to its own virtual pad, and a number of its parameters can then be edited, including its pitch, tone, and velocity. The lower portion of the Redrum interface includes a step-pattern-based sequencer that can run in perfect synchronization with the tempo of your song. Within the sequencer portion of Redrum, a number of effects are available, including shuffle, dynamics, and a flam for producing a drop-stick-roll effect.

The Effects of Reason

In addition to all of the synths, Reason also includes an impressive assortment of real-time effects that will certainly come in handy when writing new songs. Following is a rundown of the effects and their relevant parameters.

The RV-7 Digital Reverb

The RV-7 is a basic digital reverb that has been included with Reason since version 1. It is a great-sounding all-around reverb that is very conservative on your CPU.

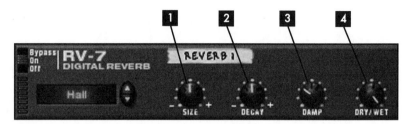

1 The Size knob adjusts the size of the room.

2 The Decay knob adjusts the length of the reverb's decay.

3 The Damp knob adjusts the equalization of the reverb effect.

4 The Dry/Wet knob adjusts the balance between a processed, or wet, signal and an unprocessed, or dry, signal.

The D-11 Foldback Distortion

The D-11 Foldback Distortion effect is a simple, yet effective, digital distortion. While not really that great for guitar tracks, it can be used to complement a bass line or perhaps a snare drum.

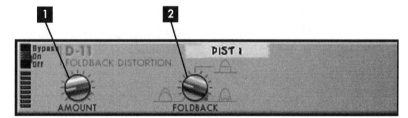

1 The Amount knob assigns the amount of distortion.

2 The Foldback knob adds character to the shape of the distortion.

The ECF-42 Envelope Controlled Filter

The ECF-42 is a combination filter/envelope generator that can be used to create pattern-controlled filter and envelope effects with any device. It should be used as an insert effect.

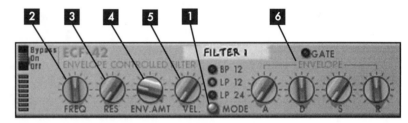

1 The Mode button switches between the different filter modes.

2 The Frequency knob adjusts the filter frequency of the ECF-42.

3 The Res knob adjusts the resonance of the filter.

4 The Envelope Amount knob determines how much the filter frequency will be affected by the triggered envelope.

5 The Velocity knob specifies how much the gate velocity affects the envelope.

6 The Envelope section is used to set the Attack, Decay, Sustain, and Release values of the envelope once it's triggered.

The PH-90 Phaser

The PH-90 is a phaser that creates a sweeping effect (kind of like a chorus effect). However, a phaser shifts portions of an audio signal out of phase, and then sends that effected signal back to the original signal, causing narrow bands of the frequency spectrum to be filtered out. The sweeping effect happens when these bands are adjusted.

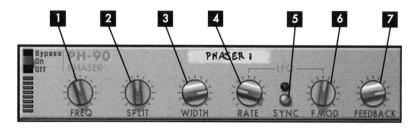

1 The Frequency knob assigns the frequency of the first notch. Once this is set, the remaining three notches move in parallel within the frequency spectrum.

2 The Split knob changes the distance between each notch, which modifies the character of the overall effect.

3 The Width knob adjusts the width of the notches.

4 The LFO Rate knob controls the modulation rate of the LFO.

5 The LFO Sync button synchronizes the LFO rate to the tempo of the Record Sequencer.

6 The LFO Frequency Modulation knob assigns the depth of LFO modulation.

7 The Feedback knob is used to alter the tone of the phaser.

The UN-16 Unison

The UN-16 is a very basic chorus effect. It produces a set number of voices that are each slightly delayed and detuned by way of low-frequency noise.

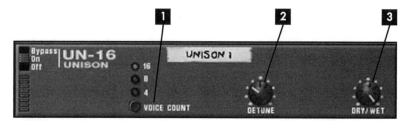

1 The Voice Count button assigns the number of voices to be produced.

2 The Detune knob increases/decreases the detuning of the individual voices.

3 The Dry/Wet knob adjusts the balance between a processed, or wet, signal and an unprocessed, or dry, signal.

The COMP-01 Compressor/Limiter

The COMP-01 is a real-time compressor that is typically used to level out audio signals that are too loud in the mix and are in danger of digitally clipping.

1 The Ratio knob sets the gain reduction of the audio signal according to the set threshold.

2 The Threshold knob sets the level that dictates when the compressor effect will be applied.

3 The Attack knob adjusts the attack of the compression effect.

4 The Release knob adjusts the length of time needed before the audio signal is unaffected by the COMP-01, once its level has fallen under the threshold.

The PEQ-2 Two-Band Parametric EQ

The PEQ-2 is a two-band parametric EQ that allows precise control over the equalization curve. While not as robust as the EQs found on the Record Main Mixer, the PEQ-2 can really come in handy when using Record on a slower computer.

1 The Frequency knob assigns the center of the EQ curve.

2 The Q knob adjusts the frequency width of the EQ curve.

3 The Gain knob boosts and cuts the gain of the EQ curve.

The BV512 Digital Vocoder

The BV512 Digital Vocoder is Reason's best effect and quite frankly one of the best vocoders I've ever had the pleasure of using. The vocoder effect is used to create robotic voices in dance and performance music and also to create a "choir of synthetic voices." Here's how it works.

A vocoder uses two separate sources of input to create a new audio signal by applying the frequency bands of one signal to the other. These two separate audio sources are known as the *carrier* and the *modulator*. The carrier can be anything that generates a constant signal, such as a string patch from the ID8, while the modulator can be anything from a vocal track to a drum loop.

These two signals are then routed to their appropriate vocoder inputs. The modulator is divided into a set number of frequency bands and then sent to an envelope follower. Meanwhile, the carrier is also divided into the same set number of frequency bands, which is then affected by the frequency bands of the modulator. This creates the vocoder effect where the carrier will have the frequency characteristics of the modulator, meaning that if the modulator gets louder, the carrier will follow. It sounds a little complicated, but it's actually pretty straightforward. If you want to hear some great examples of a vocoder, have a listen to "Around the World" by Daft Punk, or "More Bounce to the Ounce" by Zapp and Roger.

Additionally, the BV512 can be used as an equalizer. The Band switch assigns the number of filter bands, while the Equalizer/Vocoder switch is used to toggle between Vocoder mode and Equalizer mode.

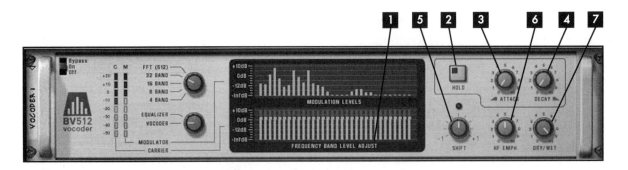

1 The Frequency Band Level adjusts the levels of the individual filter bands.

2 The Hold button freezes the current filter settings.

3 The Attack knob affects the overall attack of the frequency bands.

4 The Decay knob affects the overall decay of the frequency bands.

5 The Shift knob shifts the carrier signal filters up and down.

6 High Frequency Emphasis knob increases the high frequencies in the carrier signal.

7 Dry/Wet knob mixes between the dry signal and the wet signal.

Using the BV512 Vocoder in Record

To get some hands-on experience using a Reason device in Record, let's look at how to use the BV512 Vocoder effect. This effect uses two separate sources of input to create a new audio signal by applying the frequency bands of one signal to the other. These two separate audio sources are known as the carrier and the modulator. The *carrier* is ideally an audio source that is constantly generating sound. A good example of this is a pad playing from a Reason synth. The *modulator* is typically an audio source, such as a spoken voice or vocal track. Another typically used modulator is a drum loop for creating rhythmically enhanced sounds.

In this exercise, you'll go through the steps of routing a basic vocoding setup using a vocal track as a modulator and an instance of the Subtractor as the carrier. Before beginning, download the

Vocoder Demo song from the Cengage Learning website. Once you download the song, open it up, press the F6 key, and then the Tab key to view the back of the Device Rack.

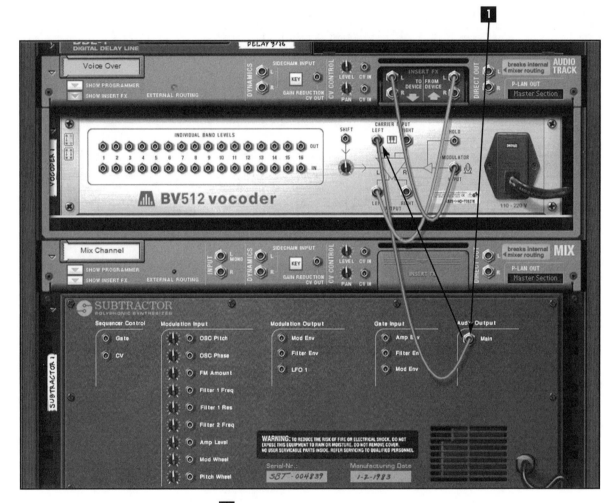

1 **Click and drag** a virtual cable **from the Main Audio Output** of the Subtractor device **to the left Carrier Input** of the BV512.

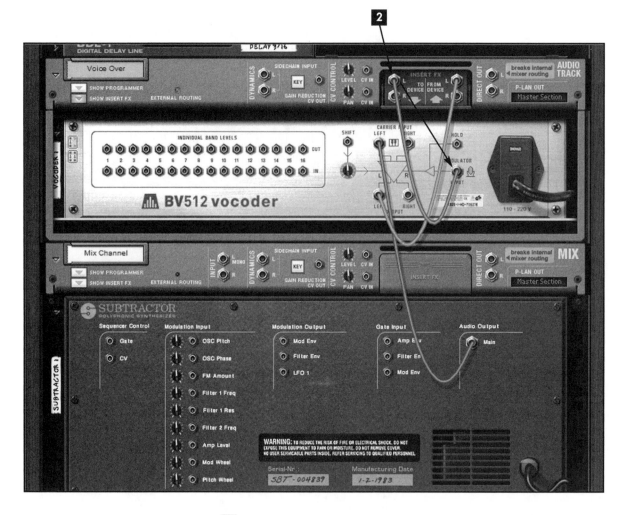

2 Click and drag a virtual cable **from the Insert FX left output** of the Audio Track device to the **Modulator Input** of the BV512.

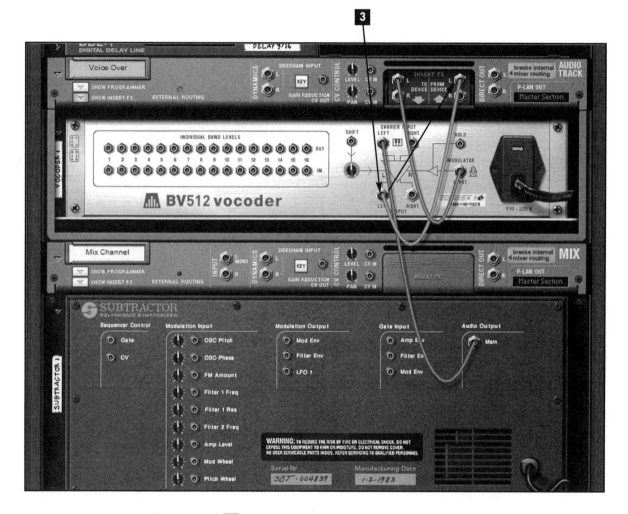

3 **Click and drag** a virtual cable **from the left audio Output** of the BV512 to the **Insert FX left input**.

Now press Play, and you will hear the vocoder effect. You can also make adjustments to the individual parameters of the BV512 to help fine-tune the effect. Press the Tab key and make the following adjustments to the BV512.

1 Set the **Dry/Wet knob** at its maximum value. This adjusts the amount of the overall vocoding effect. If you decrease the value of this parameter, you'll hear the dry vocal track, which is probably not what you want.

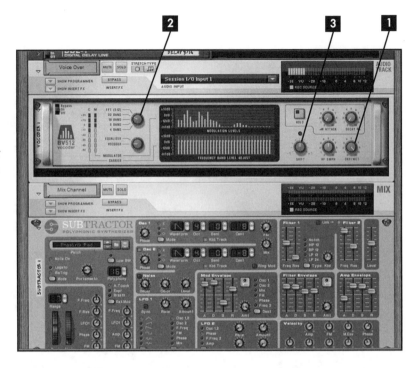

2 Set the **Band switch** to 32. This assigns the amount of bands to your vocoder. By default, this parameter is set to 16 bands, but if you adjust this to 32 bands, you'll get a much finer effect. Adjusting this parameter to 4 or 8 bands will produce a grittier effect.

3 Set the **Shift knob** to adjust the carrier signal filters up and down, which creates a sweeping effect.

As you have seen throughout the last few pages, Reason has a lot to offer Record users. Not only do you get a powerful selection of synths to use, but you also get many fantastic effects that will offer several creative possibilities for your audio tracks. Truly, using Reason and Record together is the best of both worlds.

} Index

C

D

E

Mike Seventies Guy

PZBGJNTV

Introducing *Course Clips*!

Course Clips are interactive DVD-ROM training products for those who prefer learning on the computer as opposed to learning through a book. *Course Clips Starters* are for beginners and *Course Clips Masters* are for more advanced users.

Pro Tools 8
Course Clips Master
Steve Wall ■ $49.99

Pro Tools 8
Course Clips Starter
Steve Wall ■ $29.99

Ableton Live 8
Course Clips Master
Brian Jackson ■ $49.99

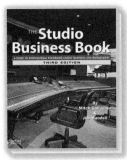

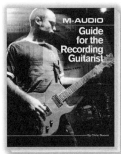

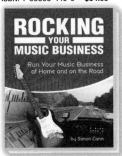